Making Contributions: An Historical Overview of Women's Role in Physics

Katherine R. Sopka

Sallie A. Watkins

Peggy A. Kidwell

Janet B. Guernsey

Lucille B. Garmon

Edited by Barbara Lotze

Papers Based on a Special Session
Sponsored by the Committee on Women in Physics
of the American Association of Physics Teachers
at the AAPT Summer Meeting,
Held in Memphis, Tennessee, in June 1983

Published by

American Association of Physics Teachers

MAKING CONTRIBUTIONS: AN HISTORICAL OVERVIEW
OF WOMEN'S ROLE IN PHYSICS

Published by:
    American Association of Physics Teachers
    Department of Physics and Astronomy
    University of Maryland
    College Park, Maryland 20742 U.S.A.

ISBN 0-917853-09-1

Contents

1. (Sopka) Frontispiece from <u>Elémens de la Philosophie</u>
<u>de Newton</u> by Voltaire (Amsterdam, 1738), showing Emilie
de Breteuil de Châtelet, translator of Newton's <u>Princi-</u>
<u>pia</u>, holding the mirror by which light from Newton is
reflected onto the writer Voltaire. (Original in the
library of the Institut für Geschichte der Naturwiss-
enschaften, Mathematik und Technik, Universität Hamburg,
kindly made available by Professor Dr. Andreas Kleinert)

2. (Sopka) Margaret Eliza Maltby. (Photo courtesy of the
M. I. T. Museum)

3. (<u>Sopka</u>) Elizabeth Rebecca Laird in the new physics laboratory, Mount Holyoke College, 1934. (Photo courtesy of AIP Niels Bohr Library)

4. (Sopka) Marie Curie at the 1911 Solvay Conference in Brussels. (Photo courtesy of AIP Niels Bohr Library)

5. (Sopka) Katharine Burr Blodgett at work in the General
Electric Research Laboratory, with her mentor, Irving Lang-
muir, and others. (Photo courtesy of the General Electric
Research and Development Center)

6. (Watkins) Lise Meitner at the Max Planck Jubilee Conference, 1958. (Photo courtesy of the AIP Niels Bohr Library)

7. (Kidwell) Cecilia Payne at Radcliffe College, 1924.
(Photo courtesy of Katherine Haramundanis)

8. (Guernsey) Formal portrait of Sarah Frances Whiting.

9. (Guernsey) Sarah Frances Whiting (left) and second-year physics students in the optics laboratory.

10. (Guernsey) Louise McDowell in New Hampshire after her retirement.

Introduction

Barbara Lotze

Allegheny College

Meadville, Pennsylvania

When asked about women's contributions to the physical sciences, most laymen--and possibly even some physicists--may come up with two or three names: Marie Curie, Lise Meitner, and perhaps Maria Goeppert-Mayer. There are few extensive studies on the topic, with Margaret Rossiter's Women Scientists in America still very much the exception. This realization prompted the Committee on Women in Physics of the American Association of Physics Teachers to sponsor a special session on "Women's Role in Physics" at the 1983 summer meeting of the organization.

In the introduction to her book, Rossiter outlines the position of women scientists in the nineteenth and early twentieth centuries:

Even as women's educational level rose and their role
outside the home expanded, they were seen as doing
only a narrow range of "womanly" activities, a stereo-
type that linked and limited them to soft, delicate,
emotional, noncompetitive, and nurturing kinds of
feelings and behavior. At the same time, the stereo-
type of "science" was seen rhetorically as almost the
opposite: tough, rigorous, rational, impersonal, masculine, competitive, and unemotional. In terms, therefore, of nineteenth-century stereotypes or rhetorical
idealizations, a woman scientist was a contradiction
in terms--such a person was unlikely to exist, and if
she did (and more and more of them were coming into
existence), she had to be "unnatural" in some way.
Women scientists were thus caught between two almost
mutually exclusive stereotypes: as scientists they
were atypical women; as women they were unusual scientists.[1]

It was the purpose of our panel to study some of those
"unusual scientists," to look at what they had contributed
to physics, and to explore the impact of social prejudice--

then and now--on their lives and on their work. The papers included in this collection are featuring various approaches to our topic. Katherine Sopka demonstrates in an historical survey spanning many centuries that women physicists are by no means a completely new phenomenon. Sallie Watkins and Peggy Kidwell deal with two outstanding female scientists-- Lise Meitner and Cecilia Payne-Gaposchkin--as examplary cases of women who devoted their lives to different fields of physics. Janet Guernsey focuses on the physics department of a particular school--Wellesley College--and on the two women who founded it and built up its continuing tradition of excellence. The concluding article by Lucille Garmon uses statistical information and other evidence to show the progress made by women in establishing themselves as not so "unusual" scientists. At the same time it becomes clear from her paper that the stereotypes mentioned by Margaret Rossiter are still with us.

While the approaches may differ and the styles of the articles reflect the individual authors, it is our hope that the mosaic provided in this publication will serve to draw more attention to the contributions made by female physicists and serve as an encouragement for women who might consider this exciting field of study.

Note

1.

   Margaret W. Rossiter, <u>Women</u> <u>Scientists</u> <u>in</u> <u>America</u>:
   <u>Struggles</u> <u>and</u> <u>Strategies</u> <u>to</u> <u>1940</u> (The Johns Hopkins
   University Press, Baltimore, 1982), p. xv.

Women Physicists in Past Generations

Katherine Russell Sopka

Fort Lewis College

Durango, Colorado

For centuries, individual women in various countries have been attracted to the study of physics. Despite limited educational and employment opportunities, some of these women have succeeded in making significant contributions to the discipline through teaching, research, or, in at least one case, translation. The lives of the dozen female physicists whose work I will discuss span some twenty-four centuries, and they represent eight countries.

Arete of Cyrene was the daughter of Aristippus, the founder of the Cyrenian school of philosophy. At his death in 356 B.C. she took over the leadership of his academy where natural and moral philosophy were taught.[1] ("Physics" became a recognized discipline only in relatively recent times; "natural philosphy," a much older term, encompassed what we now call physics, derived from the Greek word "physis" for nature.) Her teaching activities lasted for thirty-five years during which time she instructed more than one hundred students and wrote forty books. The epitaph on her grave read: "She was the splendor of Greece and possessed the beauty of Helen, the virtue of Therma, the pen of Aristippus and the tongue of Homer"--high praise in any language. After her death, the academy was continued by her son, Aristippus II, who was nicknamed "Metrodidactos"--that is, "taught by his mother."[2]

Hypatia, the daughter of Theon, the mathematician, lived from 375 to 415 A.D. and taught in Alexandria during the golden age of that city. She lectured on science and philosophy and was the inventor of several devices, such as the astrolabe and the hydroscope (for measuring the density of liquids). Her life ended at age 40 when she was stoned to death by a Christian mob for her alleged pagan beliefs.[3]

Hildegard of Bingen of twelfth-century Germany is regarded as a cosmologist by the Dictionary of Scientific Biography. In her writings, she united elements of Oriental, Judeo-Christian, and Greek cosmological ideas. But her interests and activities were broader than that. She was skilled in the medicine of her time, and she enjoyed considerable prestige in political and ecclesiastical circles. She had been a sickly child whose parents entrusted her care to Benedictine nuns. Hildegard joined that order as a young woman, subsequently rising to the rank of Superior and establishing her own convent at Bingen. As was common during that period, her writings were a blend of science, mysticism, and theology--she saw the universe as the handiwork of God. She was proposed for canonization and, although that process was apparently not formally completed, she is usually referred to as St. Hildegard. If you wish to celebrate her feast day, it is September 17.[4]

Just as Hildegard was shaped by the culture of her time, Emilie de Breteuil was clearly a product of early 18th-century France. Born into a family of minor nobility, she became upon marriage the Marquise du Châtelet. Subsequently she was a close associate (intellectually and sexually) of Voltaire. During the period of their alliance--which lasted for about fifteen years--she conducted experiments in physics, wrote a paper on "The Nature of Fire" that was published by the French Academy, and authored a book, Institutions de Physique, an up-to-date summary of the physics of her age, ostensibly for the benefit of her son, the future Marquis du Châtelet. Her best-known achievement is probably her translation of Newton's Principia Mathematica, published with her commentaries after her unfortunate death in 1749, following childbirth at age 42. Her translation of Newton's work remains the only one into the French language today.[5]

Somewhat younger than Mme. du Châtelet, but also of the 18th century, was Laura Bassi of Italy. She received a Ph.D. from the University of Bologna in 1733 and, soon after, was named a member of the faculty there, holding the chair of physics--the first woman to occupy a faculty chair at any university. Among her published writings are two treatises, one on mechanics, the other on hydrodynamics. She was well known in scholarly circles throughout Europe. (Voltaire sought, successfully, her assistance in gaining membership in the Academy of Bologna after having been turned down by the French Academy.) During her marriage to Jean-Joseph Veratti, she gave birth to twelve children. She was a devoted

mother and a pious woman. After her death in 1778, her remains were interred in the Church of Corpus Domini.[6]

As we move closer to our own time, <u>Marie</u> <u>Curie</u> stands
out as the one woman scientist familiar to the general public. The details of her life have not only been recorded by
at least two biographers, one of them her daughter Eve, but
they also have been dramatized for film and television audi-
ences.

She was born in Poland in 1867 as Maria Sklodowska, but
her scientific education and professional life took place in
France where she was known as Madame Marie Curie, wife of
physicist Pierre Curie. Her first Nobel Prize, in physics,
shared with her husband and with Henri Becquerel, was awarded in 1903 for their work in the study of natural radioactivity. Her second, in chemistry, was given to her alone in
1911. A widow at that time, she paid homage to her late husband in her acceptance address at the Nobel ceremony.

Accompanying her to Stockholm on that occasion was her
daughter, Irene, who would, twenty-four years later, return
as <u>Irene</u> <u>Joliot-Curie</u> to accept the Prize herself, together

with her husband, Frederic Joliot-Curie, for their artificial production of radioactivity.

During her lifetime, which held many trials and sorrows as well as rewards, Marie Curie was recognized throughout the world for her scientific achievements, yet she appears as a lonely figure. She participated in all of the early Solvay Congresses on Physics. In each of the group pictures taken at those conferences, she is the lone woman among two dozen men, all leaders of the international community of physicists--clear evidence of her unique position in the world of early 20th-century physics.[7]

Readers of Robert Reid's biography of Marie Curie may recall his reference to Hertha Ayrton, a British friend of hers who also was a physicist. (Following her difficult year of 1911, Marie and her daughters, traveling incognito, took refuge at Hertha's home for several months, thereby regaining emotional and physical strength.)

Hertha Ayrton lived from 1854 to 1923. She was the daughter of a Jewish family from Poland that had come to England as political refugees from the czarist regime. She studied at Girton College, a women's school located in Cambridge but not part of Cambridge University at that time. She married William Ayrton, an established physicist, and collaborated in some of his work. But she soon demonstrated competence in her own right with a laboratory set up in her home. She did original research on the electric arc, water vortices, and sand ripples, and she was invited to lecture before learned societies in England and France. In 1906 she was awarded the Hughes Medal of the Royal Society, but her candidacy for fellowship in that body was turned down. "The candidate being a married woman is not qualified for election," ruled the Society's counsel. Her book, The Electric Arc, summarized her own work and that of others and became the textbook on that topic during the period--it even had an American edition. After her husband's death in 1908, she became very active in the British women's suffrage movement, and during the First World War, she assisted the war effort by developing the "Ayrton Fan," to be used by men in the trenches under gas attack.[8]

Another noteworthy physicist was an American, Margaret Maltby. After attending Oberlin College and the Massachusetts Institute of Technology (as it is now known), she was awarded an MIT fellowship to study in Europe. In 1895, she became the first American woman to receive a Ph.D. from the University of Göttingen and the first woman to get a doctorate in physics in the history of that institution. The research for her dissertation, carried out under the direction of Woldemar Voigt, was highly esteemed by him. She stayed on for a year of postdoctoral work, funded by the Association of Collegiate Alumnae.[9] Two years later she returned to Europe at the invitation of Friedrich Kohlrausch to be his research assistant in his new position as head of the Physikalisch-Technische Reichsanstalt. The results of their collaboration on aqueous solutions were published in Wissenschaftliche Abhandlungen.

In 1900, soon after returning to the United States, she joined the faculty of Barnard College. She was the first woman physicist to attain starred status in American Men of Science, signifying that she was one of the top one thousand American contributors to science. Miss Maltby[10] was appointed associate professor and head of the physics department at Barnard in 1913 and remained in that post until her retirement in 1931. Teaching and administrative duties at Barnard and her devoted service to the American Association of University Women (as the Association of Collegiate Alumnae was renamed) left her little time for research. Her students greatly admired her. As one of them wrote me: "Professor Maltby was my mentor--a gracious lady--a friend and a counselor. Her most memorable advice to me was not to forego marriage for a career--which advice I followed and lived happily ever after."[11] Miss Maltby herself never married but nevertheless enjoyed some of the pleasures of motherhood and grandmotherhood through the adoption in 1901 of the orphaned son of a close friend.[12]

Elizabeth Laird was born in Canada in 1874. Her bachelor's degree was conferred by the University of Toronto in 1896, following which she pursued graduate studies at Bryn Mawr College, earning her Ph.D. in mathematics and physics in 1901. From 1901 until her retirement in 1940, she was associated with Mount Holyoke College, a women's school with strong emphasis on science which had evolved from Mount Holyoke Seminary, founded in the 1830s.

Miss Laird was always active in research. Her first published paper, an experimental and theoretical discussion of the period of a wire vibrating in a liquid, appeared in the *Physical Review* in 1898. Later she became best known for her work on the region of the spectrum generally referred to as "Entladungsstrahlen" which lies between the ultraviolet and x-ray regions.

Miss Laird studied in Europe on four separate occasions--the first in Berlin in 1898-99, the second and third at the Cavendish Laboratory in 1905 and 1909, and the fourth in Würzburg in 1913-14. In Würzburg her work was guided by Wilhelm Wien whom she had met the previous spring when he gave a series of lectures on theoretical physics at Columbia University. Wien was interested in the results of her spark discharge studies and arranged to have them published in the *Annalen der Physik*, but completion of this work was precluded by the outbreak of the First World War.

Throughout her professional life, Miss Laird kept up with new developments. Upon retirement from Mount Holyoke in 1941, she returned to Canada to join a radar project sponsored by the Canadian National Research Council. After the war she began to teach herself enough biophysics to be able to contribute to the work of the Ontario Cancer Research Foundation in the area of medical uses of radar wavelength radiation.[13]

The career of <u>Katharine</u> <u>Blodgett</u> differs in many respects from those of the women previously considered here. She became the first woman scientist at the Ph.D. level to be employed by the General Electric Company. She worked for that organization from 1918 to her retirement in 1963, with a two-year leave of absence being granted for her doctoral studies.

Miss Blodgett received a B.A. degree in physics from Bryn Mawr College in 1917 and a master's degree from the University of Chicago a year later. As a member of the research staff at General Electric, she was closely associated with Irving Langmuir, 1932 Nobel Prize winner in chemistry. Langmuir encouraged her to pursue further graduate study with Ernest Rutherford at the Cavendish Laboratory. Her Ph.D. in physics, attained in 1926, was the first ever to be awarded to a woman by Cambridge University. After returning to the G.E. Research Laboratory, she resumed her work with Langmuir, initially on improving the tungsten filaments of electric bulbs. Later, her most notable research dealt with thin films, leading to the development of non-reflecting glass and an extremely accurate thickness measuring device. In addition to the many awards she received for her work as a scientist, Katharine Blodgett was also honored for her civic contributions by the city of Schenectady which celebrated "Katharine Blodgett Day" in 1951 during which she was hailed "as a tireless and disciplined worker, as a cheerful and witty colleague, as a leading citizen with a social conscience and a deep sense of civic responsibility."[14]

Let us conclude this review of the accomplishments of selected women physicists with a few words about Maria Goeppert-Mayer, who did her doctoral work at the University of Göttingen with Max Born at the time when quantum mechanics was being developed. She came to the United States in 1930 as the bride of Joseph Mayer, an American chemist who had gone to Göttingen on a postdoctoral fellowship. For many years she could not find any real professional status at the institutions which employed her husband (the Johns Hopkins University, Columbia University, and the University of Chicago). But during all those years she was informally active in teaching and research and was valued as an intellectual colleague by members of the community of outstanding physicists, including Harold Urey, Edward Teller, and Enrico Fermi.

In the 1930s, she undertook, at Fermi's suggestion, the problem of predicting the valence-shell structure of the transuranic elements that were then under discussion but had not yet been produced. It later became clear that her results predicted their chemical behavior with remarkable accuracy. Her subsequent work on the shell model of the nucleus, using the concept of spin-orbit coupling, also influenced by discussions with Fermi, resulted in her being awarded a share in the 1963 Nobel Prize in Physics, together with Hans Jensen of Heidelberg.[15] Although they had initially worked completely independently, unaware of each other's research, they later became active collaborators.

It was not until 1960, when Maria Goeppert-Mayer was 54 years old, that she was finally appointed a full professor at a major university, the University of California at San Diego which offered positions to both her and her husband. Unfortunately, her health declined and she was never able to enjoy the full potential of her new position. She died in 1972.[16]

I believe that each of the twelve women considered in this paper could serve to dispel the myth that women "can't do" or "don't belong in" physics.[17] While it is true that they have been in the past, and continue to be even today, a small minority of the physics profession and have been subject to additional outside social restrictions, it is impressive how much each was able to accomplish within the social and intellectual context of her time. Women physicists have needed not only to be intellectually capable, but also to have personalities that would enable them to follow what was often a lonely path, whether they were married or not.

Let me conclude by expressing my pleasure with the initiative taken by the American Association of Physics Teachers in calling attention to the roles played by women in the past, thereby heightening our collective awareness of the potential for future contributions to physics by women entering the field who may be in our classrooms today. We cannot help but be optimistic that, with the elimination of many barriers from the past, women physicists of future generations will be more numerous and will participate more fully in the world of physics.

Notes

1.

H.J. Mozans, <u>Women in Science</u> (D. Appleton Co., New York, 1913; quoted here from the paperback reprint, MIT Press, 1974), pp. 197-199. Note: "Mozans" was a pseudonym used by Father John A. Zahm, a priest associated with Notre Dame University, according to Michael J. Crowe, "Who Was H.J. Mozans?", Isis <u>68</u> (1977), 111.

2.

George Sarton, <u>A History of Science: Hellenistic Science and Culture in the Last Three Centuries B.C.</u> (Harvard University Press, Cambridge, 1949), p.100.

3.

Edna E. Kramer, <u>A History of Scientific Biography</u>, Vol. 6, edited by Charles C. Gillispie (Charles Scribner's Sons, New York, 1972).

<u>World's Who's Who in Science From Antiquity to the Present</u> (Marquis Who's Who, Inc., Chicago, 1968).

Also: Mozans, <u>op. cit.</u>, pp. 199-201, and Sarton, <u>op. cit.</u>, p. 34.

4.

Walter Pagel, "Hildegard of Bingen," Dictionary of Scientific Biography, Vol. 6, pp. 396-398.

The Catholic Encyclopedia (The Encyclopedia Press, Inc., New York, 1910), pp. 351-353.

Lynn Thorndike, A History of Magic and Experimental Science During the First Thirteen Centuries of Our Era, Vol. 2 (Columbia University Press, New York, 1923), pp. 124-154.

George Sarton, Introduction to the History of Science, Vol. 2 (The Williams and Wilkins Co. for the Carnegie Institution of Washington, Baltimore, 1931), pp. 386-388.

I have also profited from helpful discussions with medieval historian, Professor Thomas R. Eckenrode.

5.

Rene Taton, "Châtelet, Gabrielle-Emilie le Tonnelier de Breteuil, Marquise du," Dictionary of Scientific Biography, Vol. 3, 1971, pp. 215-217.

Mozans, op. cit., pp. 201-202.

Note: There are two full-length biographies of Madame du Châtelet: Nancy Mitford, Voltaire in Love (Harper and Bros., New York, 1957) and Samuel Edwards, The Divine Mistress (David McKay Co., Inc., New York, 1970).

6.

Mozans, op. cit., pp. 202-210.

World's Who's Who in Science.

7.

Robert Reid, Marie Curie (The New American Library, Inc., New York, 1974).

Eve Curie, Madame Curie, translated by Vincent Sheean (Pocket Books, Inc., New York, 1937).

8.

Evelyn Sharp, Hertha Ayrton 1854-1923: A Memoir (Edw. Arnold and Co., London, 1926).

Mozans, op. cit., pp. 212, 230.

9.

An interesting and informative discussion of the Association of Collegiate Alumnae and its role in enabling American women, including Maltby, to study in Europe may be found in: Margaret W. Rossiter, Women Scientists in America: Struggles and Strategies to 1940 (The Johns Hopkins University Press, Baltimore, 1982).

10.

American women physicists of her generation were usually referred to as "Miss," regardless of their doctoral or professional status. Very few were married. In the 1940s, a dean at Radcliffe College told me, "In my days, society expected celibacy of women scholars."

11.

Author's File, July 5, 1977.

12.

Agnes Townsend Wiebusch, "Maltby, Margaret Eliza," Notable American Women, Vol.2 (Belknap Press of Harvard University, Cambridge, 1971).

E. Scott Barr, "Maltby, Margaret Eliza," Am.J.Phys. 28 (1960), 474-475.

"Margaret E. Maltby, Pioneer," J.Am.Ass.Univ.Women 1944, 245-246.

13.

E.R. Laird, "Autobiographical Notes," deposited at the Center for History of Physics, American Institute of Physics, New York.

14.

Bryn Mawr College Notes, June 5, 1960, Citation for Distinguished Service awarded to Katharine Burr Blodgett.

G.L. Gaines, Jr., "In Memoriam: Katharine Burr Blodgett 1898-1979," and "On the History of Langmuir-Blodgett

Films," reprints supplied to me by George Wise of the General Electric Research and Development Center. I am also indebted to Ruth Shoemaker of the G.E. Photographic Unit who kindly provided me with photographs of Katharine Blodgett.

15.

The Nobel Prize in Physics in 1963 was awarded half to Eugene Wigner, the other half shared by Goeppert-Mayer and Jensen.

16.

Joan Dash, "Maria Goeppert-Mayer," in A Life of One's Own (Harper and Row, New York, 1973), pp. 229-346.

17.

Vera Kistiakowsky, "Women in Physics: Unnecessary, Injurious and Out of Place?" Phys. Today 33 (Feb. 1980), 32-40.

Lise Meitner's Scientific Legacy

Sallie A. Watkins

University of Southern Colorado

Pueblo, Colorado

Following her hasty flight from Nazi Germany to Sweden, Lise Meitner wrote to her former colleague, Otto Hahn: "One point which has not yet been discussed in detail is the question of my scientific 'legacy.' From my point of view, this is a central concern."[1] The discussion below will set forth the Meitner legacy. It will present accounts of the many contributions of Lise Meitner to physics, in particular to the field of nuclear physics. Where her work overlapped or complemented that of others, historical perspectives of the interplay will be dealt with.

Lise Meitner's scientific work began with the experiments she conducted for her doctoral dissertation. The official record of approval of this thesis, preserved in the

archives at the University of Vienna,[2] indicates that she
"verified a formula of Maxwell's." The work was done under
the supervision of Franz Exner and consisted of a study of
heat conduction in inhomogeneous materials. The measurements
were made on several mercury ointments. Her dissertation was
approved on November 28, 1905. It was published in 1906.[3]

Meitner stayed at the University of Vienna until 1907,
doing postdoctoral research. Otto Frisch, her nephew,
writes, "When she succeeded in clearing up a point concerning optical reflexion which had puzzled Lord Rayleigh she
was encouraged to think of a career in theoretical physics.
. . ."[4] The paper reporting the results of this work was
published in 1906.[5] During the period of her postdoctoral
work in Vienna, she was also introduced to the new field of
radioactivity--this by Stefan Meyer. At the time, it was not
known whether or not alpha rays are deflected in passing
through matter. Lise Meitner designed and carried out one of
the first experiments to show that some deflection does, in
fact, occur.[6]

After the death of Ludwig Boltzmann, head of the Department of Physics at the University of Vienna, Max Planck

was invited to visit the department as a candidate to suc-
ceed Boltzmann. Lise Meitner was so much impressed by Planck
that she decided to go to Berlin to attend his lectures and
to do experimental work. Here she met a young chemist, Otto
Hahn, who was searching for a physicist to work with him in
his research on radioactivity. They formed an alliance which
lasted for thirty years.

In 1907, Meitner published another single-author paper
on alpha radiation.[7]

1908 saw the publication of three papers by the Meitner-Hahn team.[8-10] In October 1907, their first joint un-
dertaking had been a study of beta-ray energies. (This puzzling issue was to trouble Meitner until 1930. A detailed
historical account of her work on beta-radiation appears in
The American Journal of Physics.[11]) The 1908 Meitner-Hahn
papers reported the results of their early beta-radiation
studies as well as the discovery of a new short-lived product of actinium. They called it Actinium C.

The 1909 papers by Meitner and Hahn show them continuing their work on beta rays, announcing a new method of

preparation for radioactive decay products, and beginning to focus on particular elements, namely radium and thorium.[12-17]

By 1910, Lise Meitner had achieved professional acceptance as a research physicist in the field of radioactivity. In his autobiography, Otto Hahn writes of these years: "Lise Meitner and I were taken seriously by the physicists; I have already mentioned the friendly atmosphere among my colleagues, younger ones as well as those of my own age. I also got along well with the chemists--partly, I think, because my very different line of research did not compete with the research done by the many Privatdozents who worked in Fischer's Institute."[18] Meitner, for her part, had defined a comfortable working relationship with Hahn. All that was missing was a salary! Hahn writes:

Of course Lise Meitner could not become a Privatdozent; at that time there were no female professors of any rank in Berlin. But in 1912 Planck took the step of making her an "assistant" at the Institute for Theoretical Physics of the University of Berlin. I think she was one of the first female scientific assistants in all Prussia. She retained this position for three years.[19]

In August 1914, the First World War began. Hahn was immediately drafted into the reserves. Lise Meitner took a course in roentgenology and human anatomy at the City Hospital in Lichterfelde, just outside of Berlin. She then volunteered for service as an x-ray technician in the Austrian army.

In the fall of 1917, Meitner and Hahn were in a position to resume their work. They set about searching for the parent substance of actinium. By March 1918, they had isolated and named a new element, protactinium. (It was later shown that a substance discovered by Kasimir Fajans and O. Göhring and called by them "brevium" was a short-lived isotope of protactinium. At the time, Frederick Soddy's concept of isotopes was not yet known in Germany.) The announcement of the discovery of protactinium by Meitner and Hahn in 1918[20] was the beginning of a series of papers by them on the properties and behavior of that element.

In 1918, Lise Meitner finally received a professional appointment. She became the head of the Physical-Radioactive

Department at the Kaiser Wilhelm Institute for Chemistry. For four years, she divided her time between administrative duties and the completion of the studies on protactinium. Her collaboration with Otto Hahn was interrupted because he had become interested in the study of new elements and their chemical properties, while she found it more exciting to investigate radioactive emanations. In 1922, she returned to her earlier work on beta radiation.

Although, as was mentioned earlier, her main concern was with the problem of beta-ray energies, she made several important and fundamental discoveries along the way. In 1925, she settled an argument with C.D. Ellis and H.W.B. Skinner that had lasted for years. It concerned the sequence of events in beta decay. The question was this: When a gamma ray from the nucleus gives rise to a secondary electron, does the energy transfer take place in the electron shells of the original or of the new atom? Meitner was able to show that the secondary beta rays are associated with the new atom, so the gamma radiation is emitted after the disintegration of the original atom.[21]

Otto Frisch writes of this period of her work:

She also observed and correctly interpreted the radiationless transitions in which an electron from an outer shell jumps into a vacancy in an inner shell, its energy not being radiated away as a characteristic x-ray quantum but used in eject-ing another electron. This phenomenon is usually named after Pierre Auger who described it inde-pendently and more clearly about two years later.[22]

Also in connection with their beta-ray studies, Meitner and K. Philipp were among the first to report observing pos-itrons.[23]

It is well known that the puzzling issue of the contin-uous beta-ray spectrum was not solved until Wolfgang Pauli wrote his now-famous open letter to Lise Meitner and Hans Geiger in 1930. He proposed the existence of an unobtrusive thief-particle which steals energy from the betas as they are emitted. In an unpublished lecture given at Bryn Mawr College on May 4, 1959, Lise Meitner reminded her audience that, in his letter, Pauli had used the term "neutron" for the particle "because the particle which we now call neutron had not yet been discovered."[24] She commented that, as we know, the name "neutrino" was assigned by Enrico Fermi.

Throughout her scientific career, Lise Meitner had keen insight into the modification and improvement of experimental design. Hahn writes of one of his 1909 papers, "Lise Meitner, after reading my manuscript, said immediately, 'What you have observed here with actinium and with fairly thick layers of the preparation should be far easier to observe on alpha-emitting active deposits in infinitesimally thin layers.'"[25] She was right, and her suggestion led to the joint paper of the same year already mentioned.

Of her capability for adapting methods and equipment developed by others for her own use, Frisch writes:

A rather original idea was to use Millikan's droplet method to study the ionization density of alpha particles in air along their path, which was done by her student Gerhard Schmidt (Z.Phys. 72, 275, 1931). She also introduced C.T.R. Wilson's cloud chamber, which had been hardly used since its invention in 1911, to Berlin and used it in many researches, together with her students and with her assistant Kurt Philipp, and introduced innovations such as its use at greatly reduced pressure for the study of electrons. . . .

In 1926 Hans Geiger and W. Mueller developed their wire counter, later to become known as the Geiger-Mueller counter, the most widely used instrument in nuclear physics; and Lise Meitner got a student to try it out. When the student complained about trouble from a gamma-ray source next door she immediately saw that the great sensitivity of this new instrument would make it possible to measure the attenuation of well-collimated, narrow beams of gamma-rays. Here was an opportunity to test a recently published formula by Oskar Klein and Y. Nishina relating to the Compton effect, the collisions of high-energy protons with the loosely bound electrons in matter.[26]

Meitner's work on the Klein-Nishina formula was done with H.H. Hupfeld and published in 1930.[27,28] It was in the course of these experiments that they observed the anomalous gamma-ray attenuation which later was explained as being pair production.

In 1934, Meitner and Hahn resumed serious collaboration and began the work which was to lead to Meitner's most famous contribution to the body of knowledge in physics.

Hitler had seized power in Germany in January 1933, but Lise Meitner was not affected by the anti-Semitic policies of his administration since she was an Austrian citizen. It was only when Austria was occupied by German troops in March 1938 that she was no longer protected. She tried through Fritz Bosch, President of the Kaiser Wilhelm Society, to obtain official permission to leave the country, but her attempts were unsuccessful. Then Peter Debye, a colleague of hers, wrote to his friend, Dirk Coster, at the University of Groningen in Holland, explaining the situation and seeking help. Coster and two colleagues somehow saw to it that the Dutch immigration officers would allow her to enter the Netherlands without a visa and with a worthless Austrian passport. In July 1938, Coster went to Berlin to accompany Meitner to Holland. She had only one and one-half hours to pack; the one person who knew that she was leaving the laboratory permanently was Hahn.

From the Netherlands, Meitner went on to Denmark, to

visit her close friends, Margrethe and Niels Bohr. She then went to Kungälv, near Göteborg, on the west coast of Sweden, to visit her friend, Eva von Bahr-Bergius, also a physicist. Through the intervention of Niels Bohr, it was arranged that she would have a position in Stockholm, in the laboratory of Manne Siegbahn.

The Christmas holiday of 1938 found her once again in Kungälv. Her nephew, Otto Frisch, was working in the Bohr laboratory in Copenhagen at the time, and she invited him to Kungälv to share the holiday. At their first breakfast together, Meitner was preoccupied with the contents of a letter she had just received from Otto Hahn. He reported unmistakable evidence that radioactive barium isotopes were formed from uranium bombardment. Meitner had been working with him and Fritz Strassmann[29] on this course of experiments before her hasty departure from Berlin. Frisch was reluctant to listen, wanting to discuss another experiment with her. But she was adamant. They went for a walk in the woods, he wearing cross-country skis, she running along beside. Finally, they sat down on a log. She recalled the liquid droplet model of the nucleus proposed by Gamow, he considered surface tension, suggested some numbers, she remem-bered the formula for mass-defect, did the energy calcula-tions, and it was clear to them that the uranium nucleus had been split. Meitner had to return to Stockholm and Frisch to Copenhagen. Their joint paper[30] was composed by long-distance telephone. It was in this paper that the term "nuclear fission" was used for the first time.

Lise Meitner's situation with Manne Siegbahn proved to be disappointing--a fact documented in her letters to Otto Hahn following July 1938.[31] In the spring of 1946, she was a Visiting Professor at the Catholic University of America. In 1947, she retired from the Nobel Institute and began re-search at a small laboratory set up for her by the Swedish Atomic Energy Committee. Later, she tranferred her research to a laboratory of the Royal Academy for Engineering Sci-ences. In 1954, we find her writing to Karl Herzfeld, Chair-man of the Department of Physics at the Catholic University of America, "When your first letter came I was just about--because of my age--to dissolve my own Nuclear Physics De-partment and to move to Docent Eklund's Department, where I have got so to say an 'old age room.'"[32] (In a footnote she added, "very comfortable.") Yet, the spring of 1959 found her again lecturing in the United States, at Bryn Mawr College.

Finally, in 1960, she did retire, this time to Cambridge, England. She had several relatives in that section of the country.

During her lifetime as an active physicist, Lise Meitner published more than 140 scientific papers. These remain in the literature of physics; collected, they form her "Scientific Legacy."

Acknowledgments

Deep gratitude is owed to the following for making available materials essential to the preparation of this manuscript: Dr. Rolf Neuhaus, Archives of the Max Planck Institute; Dr. Auguste Dick, Physics Library, University of Vienna; Dr. Al Albano, Bryn Mawr College; Dr. James Brennan, Catholic University of America; Ms. Marion Stewart, Churchill College Archives; and the family of Dr. Lise Meitner.

Notes

1.

L. Meitner to O. Hahn, Sept. 9, 1938. Original preserved in the archives of the Max-Planck-Institut, Berlin-Dahlem.

2.

Protocol Number 1964.

3.

L. Meitner, "Wärmeleitung in inhomogenen Körpern." II. Phys. Inst. Wien, Bd. 115, Abt. IIa, 125.

4.

O. Frisch, Biographical Memoirs of Fellows of the Royal Society 16, November, 1970, 406.

5.

L. Meitner, "Über einige Folgerungen, die sich aus den Fresnel'schen Reflexionsformeln ergeben." S. Ber. Preuss. Akad. Wiss.; Math. Naturwiss. Klasse 115, Abt. IIa, June 1906.

6.

L. Meitner. Phys. Z. 7, 588 (1906).

7.

L. Meitner. Ibid., 8, 489 (1907).

8.

O. Hahn, L. Meitner. Ibid., 9, 321 (1908).

9.

O. Hahn, L. Meitner. Ibid., 9, 649 (1908).

10.

O. Hahn, L. Meitner. Ibid., 9, 697 (1908).

11.

S. Watkins. Am. Jour. Phys. 51, 6 (1983).

12.

O. Hahn, L. Meitner. Verh. dt. phys. Ges. 11, 55 (1909).

13.

O. Hahn, L. Meitner. Ibid., 11, 648 (1909).

14.

O. Hahn, L. Meitner. Phys. Z. 10, 422 (1909).

15.

O. Hahn, L. Meitner. Ibid., 10, 697 (1909).

16.

O. Hahn, L. Meitner. Ibid., 10, 741 (1909).

17.

O. Hahn, L. Meitner. Ibid., 10, 948 (1909).

18.

Otto Hahn, A Scientific Autobiography (Charles Scribner's Sons, New York, 1966), p. 81.

19.

Ibid., p. 66.

20.

O. Hahn, L. Meitner. Phys. Z. 19, 208 (1918).

21.

L. Meitner. Z. Phys. 34, 807 (1925).

22.

O. Frisch, op. cit., p. 409.

23.

Ibid.

24.

L. Meitner, "The Early History of Radioactivity" (Unpublished Lecture). Archives of the Department of Physics, Bryn Mawr College, Bryn Mawr, Pennsylvania.

25.

O. Hahn, op. cit., p. 61.

26.

O. Frisch, op. cit., p. 409.

27.

L. Meitner, H.H. Hupfeld. Phys. Z. 31, 947 (1930).

28.

L. Meitner, H.H. Hupfeld. Naturwissensch. 18, 534

(1930).

29.

F. Krafft, Im Schatten der Sensation: Leben und Wirken von Fritz Strassmann (Verlag Chemie, Weinheim, 1981).

30.

O. Frisch, L. Meitner. Nature 143, 239 (1939).

31.

Originals preserved in the archives of the Max-Planck-Institut, Berlin-Dahlem.

32.

Original preserved in the archives of the Department of Physics, Catholic University of America, Washington, D.C.

Cecilia Payne-Gaposchkin: The Making of an Astrophysicist

Peggy A. Kidwell

Smithsonian Institution

Washington, D.C.

This article will examine several aspects of the life and work of Cecilia Payne-Gaposchkin, a woman who was not a physicist but an astrophysicist. Payne was born in England in 1900 and studied physics as well as astronomy as an undergraduate at Cambridge University. She came to the United States in 1923 for a year's postgraduate study at the Harvard College Observatory. Here she promptly began an investigation of the temperature and composition of stellar atmospheres that secured her the first Ph.D. in astronomy granted by Radcliffe College, a permanent post at the Harvard College Observatory, and an international reputation as an astrophysicist. Payne remained at Harvard for her entire career, achieving, at the ripe age of 56, a promotion from a lectureship to the rank of professor of astronomy, the first woman ever to be promoted to the rank of professor at Harvard. Payne-Gaposchkin wrote seven books as well as an autobiography and a host of technical papers and was quite probably the most eminent woman astronomer of all time. She married the Russian-born astronomer Sergei Gaposchkin in 1933 and mothered three children. In 1979, she died in Lexington, Massachusetts.[1]

In this essay, I will consider three questions that relate to Payne-Gaposchkin's early career. These may be summarized rather crudely as follows: First, how did Payne's education prepare her for a career in science? Second, why did she leave England to go to the Harvard College Observatory? Finally, what did she do when she got there? To answer these questions, I have used Payne-Gaposchkin's publications, her autobiography and correspondence, and interviews with several people who knew her.

First, then, how was Payne educated? Her parents, an historian and a painter, believed that their children should have the training needed by professionals. Cecilia, who wanted to study science, her brother, who became an archeologist, and her sister, who was to be an architect, all received an early dose of the classics, modern languages, and mathematics. Thus Payne spent six years at a small school in the London suburbs where she learned reading, writing, mathematics, French, German, and Latin. She then attended a London girls' school and was trained particularly in classical languages and religion. Indeed, many years later, when a friend inquired about the classics curriculum at Tufts University, Payne reported that the entire undergraduate program there did not include as much material as she had studied as a schoolgirl![2]

In her popular writings, Payne would make good use of her extensive training in literature. However, she had decided early on that she wanted to be a scientist, and she yearned for better courses in German, mathematics, chemistry, botany, and physics. Finally, in 1918, she transferred to St. Paul's Girls' School. As she put it, it was like going from the Middle Ages into modern times. The school provided both well-trained teachers and excellent laboratories; by the end of the year, Cecilia won a scholarship to study natural sciences at Newnham College of Cambridge University. At that time, women could attend Cambridge, although they would not be granted degrees there until the 1940s.

Even though Payne knew that she wanted to study science, she was not sure which science it would be. In her first year at Cambridge, she signed up for a program of botany, chemistry, and physics, with the greatest emphasis on physics. This combination may sound odd, but Payne then planned to become a schoolteacher, and botany, chemistry, and physics were the sciences most often taught in British girls' schools in those years.[3]

Her careful plans went awry early in her first year. Cambridge's leading physicist, Ernest Rutherford, gave her the distinct impression that he was not interested in women students. Moreover, Payne heard the astronomer Arthur S. Eddington lecture on his eclipse expedition to the island of Principe and its implications for Einstein's general theory of relativity. She was enormously impressed by Eddington's talk and decided to make astrophysics her life's work. While continuing her courses in other subjects, she attended as many astronomy classes as her schedule allowed. She also set the telescope at Newnham College in working order and presided over the institution's Science Society.

By the time Payne finished her education at Cambridge, she had published one research paper and been elected to Britain's Royal Astronomical Society. According to a fellow student, she was "very keen" in her work, and she had warm recommendations from her professors.[4] Why should she leave England?

Unfortunately, her native country offered no opportunities for women who wanted to earn their living as research astronomers and astrophysicists. To understand better the choices Payne had, I have examined the careers of 257 women who participated in British astronomy during the first three decades of this century. Most of these women were members of astronomical societies, particularly the largely amateur British Astronomical Association. As far as I can tell, most had not attended any university. About one quarter of the women found employment in writing popular treatises on astronomy, performing routine calculations at observatories, or teaching in schools and universities. Several other women carried on an old British tradition and worked as voluntary assistants in the observatories of their male friends and relatives. None was a research astronomer and none had a teaching post in astronomy.

The situation of these British women differed in two important ways from that of their American contemporaries. First, they could not obtain the usual credentials of professional astronomers. Rising British astronomers traditionally studied mathematics and mathematical physics at Cambridge and completed their formal training as assistants at major observatories or directors of colonial observing stations. Women had been able to study at Cambridge University from the 1870s. However, contemporary records suggest that women were uniformly barred from observing positions and hence had to depend for their training on the experience with telescopes they had gained as undergraduates and as amateur astronomers. Graduate degrees were only gaining ground very slowly in the 1920s. In the United States, on the other hand, women had received doctorates in astronomy as early as 1894, and they could pick from among several graduate programs.

Secondly, the demand for women trained in astronomy was greater in the United Sates than in Britain. This reflects not only the general growth of American astronomy but also national customs. Observatories in both countries hired computers to carry out routine calculations. (At this time, computers were people, not machines.) By 1920, many if not most of the computers at American observatories were women. However, British observatories had long hired teenaged boys to do this work, and they would continue to do so into the 1930s. American women astronomers also worked at women's colleges, where they had their own observatories, trained students, and sometimes carried out research programs. On the other hand, when British women's colleges hired tutors to assist students taking astronomy, they were hiring people to help with mathematics and physics courses. They employed mathematicians and physicists, not astronomers. Of five women holding doctorates who participated in the British astronomical community before 1930, only Payne would become a research astronomer. The others taught physics, mathematics, and biochemistry.[5]

Under these circumstances, Payne's search for a job was, as one friend put it, a "gallant but anxious enterprise."[6] A fellow student suggested that she might have better opportunities in the United States, and Payne took the idea seriously. When Harlow Shapley of the Harvard College Observatory lectured in London, she asked him if she could come and study with him. Shapley was just starting a graduate program at Radcliffe and offered her a fellowship. Combining this with funds from Newnham College, Payne was able to plan a year's stay at Harvard.[7]

To turn to my final question: what did Payne do once she arrived at Harvard? In general, she threw herself into research. Payne relished the New England climate, enjoyed long talks with Shapley and other astronomers, and, most especially, treasured her freedom. She later recalled that it was a great pleasure to do just as much astronomy as she wished, without having lectures to attend or classwork to worry about. She could study as late as she pleased, with no rules about when the lights went out. As she put it, "for a bit, I almost worked night and day without stopping, it was marvelous."[8]

Specifically, Payne set out to give a physical interpretation of the existing classification of stellar spectra. In the previous thirty years, women at Harvard had examined the spectra of hundreds of thousands of stars. They found that these spectra could be divided into seven broad classes according to the relative intensity of various absorption

lines. Developments in atomic physics and statistical mechanics allowed the Indian physicist M.N. Saha to suggest
that changes in the degree of ionization of stellar atmospheres, and hence observed differences in spectra.[9] Payne
hoped to use the photographic plates at Harvard and Saha's
theory to develop a general description of stellar atmospheres and a temperature scale for these regions.

As Payne set about this work, she encountered several
fundamental problems. First, she had never previously measured and interpreted spectra, and she found the Harvard
plates difficult to use at best. Diligence and a certain
amount of coaching from her colleagues helped her to over-
come this problem. Secondly, soon after her arrival, Donald
H. Menzel came to Harvard. Menzel, a graduate student at
Princeton, wanted to work on precisely the same problem that
interested Payne. Harlow Shapley decided to divide the problem between them, assigning hotter stars to Payne ad cooler
ones to Menzel.[10] As one might expect, this compromise left
both students dissatisfied. A third problem was more mundane. Payne had been granted a fellowship for only one year.
A timely grant from the American Association of University
Women made possible a second year's study.

According to the ionization theory developed from Saha's work, all stars were chemically alike. Differences in temperature and pressure of stellar atmospheres caused differences in the ionization of their atoms and hence in stellar spectra. Payne carefully collected observations of changes in the intensity of various spectral lines from one spectral class to the next. Knowing the class at which absorption lines due to a given element reached maximum intensity, knowing the energy required to ionize atoms of the element, and estimating the pressure, she deduced the temperature of the stellar atmosphere in question. Accumulating data for several elements and several spectral classes, she arrived at a temperature scale for stellar atmospheres.

After Payne's first year at Harvard, Menzel left to take a job at the University of Iowa, and she was free to extend her work to stars of all spectral classes. At this time, she also wondered what ionization theory implied about the relative abundance of elements in stellar atmospheres. What was the chemical composition of the stars? Astronomers believed that the composition of stellar atmospheres resembled that of the earth's crust. Two British theorists had recently pointed out that the spectral class at which lines of an element first become visible depended, in part, on the abundance of the element. Assuming that the temperature was known, they showed how to calculate abundances from these observations of marginal appearances. Payne had accumulated the necessary data, and, in the fall of 1924, wrote a paper on the subject.

Her paper demonstrated the thoroughness that would mark her entire work. An earlier astronomer, H.H. Plaskett, had used scattered observations of the marginal appearances of a few elements to deduce abundances. Payne examined a relatively homogeneous collection of spectra, all studied by a single observer. In her calculations, she used the stellar temperature scale she had deduced from ionization theory. Moreover, she obtained data on twenty of the twenty-five most abundant elements in the earth's crust.

Payne's results were startling. To be sure, atoms of silicon, carbon, and common metals occurred in about the same relative numbers in stellar atmospheres as on earth. However, helium was far more abundant in the stars. Moreover, hydrogen atoms, which in the earth's crust were about three times more abundant than atoms of a common metal like aluminum, were apparently one million times more abundant in stellar atmospheres. In short, Payne's results suggested that stellar atmospheres were composed primarily of hydrogen and helium, with traces of other elements.

Shapley sent Payne's manuscript off to Henry Norris Russell in Princeton, who, at first glance, thought that it seemed "a very good thing."[11] On further reflection, Russell concluded, "It is clearly impossible that hydrogen should be a million times more abundant than the metals." Russell went on to suggest that an idea he had developed with Karl Compton might help to explain the apparent high abundance of hydrogen in the stars. He did not know how his argument would apply to helium.[12]

Neither the original draft of Payne's paper nor any account of her reaction to Russell's letter has survived. We do know that she greatly respected Russell and feared his power among astronomers. Indeed, she wrote a friend at this time that "the fate of such as I could be sealed by him with a word."[13] In view of this attitude, the conclusions of an article she sent to the Proceedings of the National

Academy of Sciences in early February of 1925 are not sur-
prising. Here she presented her calculations of the relative
abundance of the elements in stellar atmospheres. However,
she commented that the abundances deduced for hydrogen and
helium were "improbably high" and "almost certainly not
real." She said, just as Russell had suggested, that Russell's and Compton's work might explain the great apparent
abundance of hydrogen, and that helium remained a problem.
Thus, although her data indicated that the composition of
stars differed radically from that of the earth, she accepted Russell's authority and argued that the stars were funda-
mentally like the earth's crust.[14]

Payne drew together her studies of stellar temperatures, spectral classification, and the relative abundance
of the elements in a thesis entitled Stellar Atmospheres: A
Contribution to the Observational Study of High Temperatures
in the Reversing Layers of Stars. This monograph, published
by the Harvard College Observatory in the summer of 1925,
established her reputation as an astronomer.[15] E.F. Carpenter read the book on a summer drive through Texas and reported that "'Stellar atmospheres' makes the desert seem
cooler."[16] Russell wrote Shapley that it was the best doc-

toral thesis he had ever read, with the possible exception of Shapley's own thesis.[17] Thirty-seven years later, Otto Struve and Velta Zeburgs wrote in their history of twentieth-century astronomy: "It is undoubtedly the most brilliant Ph.D. thesis ever written in astronomy."[18] On a more mundane level, Shapley was not sure that as many as a hundred astronomers and physicists would spend $ 2.50 for a book by a young astrophysicist.[19] He was delighted to report later that the entire edition of six hundred copies had sold out within three years.[20]

Stellar Atmospheres was, as one reviewer put it, "at the same time an attractive story and a work of reference."[21] Payne divided her book into three parts. The first section was a systematic exposition of atomic physics as it pertained to the origin of line spectra, and of the physics of stellar atmospheres, independent of Saha's theory. Here she supplied both necessary background for those unfamiliar with stellar spectroscopy, and a valuable summary of recent data for experts in the field.

In the second part of Stellar Atmospheres, Payne presented her physical interpretation of stellar spectra. After a general description of the excitation and ionization of atoms of a hot gas, she outlined the assumptions and relevant mathematical consequences of the most recent version of Saha's ionization theory. She also gave her own data on the relative intensity of the lines produced by neutral atoms of thirteen elements and by ionized states of atoms of eleven elements. Noting the spectral class at which each of these lines reached maximum intensity and calculating the temperature at this maximum, she obtained a temperature scale for stellar atmospheres.

In the final and shortest section of her book, Payne discussed the relative abundance of elements in stellar atmospheres, presenting data and calculations from her 1925 paper. As before, she dismissed her results for hydrogen and helium as "almost certainly not real." Russell's and Compton's work might possibly explain the observed abundance of hydrogen, she said, but helium remained a mystery. The puzzle Payne proposed would trouble astrophysicists until 1929 when Henry Norris Russell himself would argue persuasively that in fact the sun consisted primarily of hydrogen and helium.[22]

More generally, at the close of Stellar Atmospheres, Payne affirmed her belief that in astrophysics, "observation must make the way for theory, and only if it does can the science have its greatest productivity."[23] Her thesis amply demonstrated how empirical classification and rough measurement might pave the way to an understanding of stellar atmospheres. The subject of her research would change with the years, but observation, preferably as it pertained to current theory, retained its central place.

In closing, I would like to recount one episode from much later in Payne-Gaposchkin's life. As noted earlier, she was finally made a full professor at Harvard in 1956. At that time, she sent handwritten notes to all the women students in astronomy, inviting them to celebrate the occasion in the Observatory library. After appropriate flowery speeches, Payne-Gaposchkin herself rose to speak. According to one account, "she said 'I find myself in the unlikely role of a thin wedge.' It brought down the house. She (was) a very large person, but she could make fun of herself and see the humor of the whole business."[24] Payne-Gaposchkin was indeed a large woman, but, as I hope this paper has suggested, she had long experience as a thin wedge.

Notes

1.

Unless otherwise noted, details of Payne-Gaposchkin's life are taken from: Cecilia Payne-Gaposchkin: An Autobiography and Other Recollections, edited by Katherine Haramundanis (Cambridge University Press, Cambridge, U.K., 1984).

2.

C. Payne-Gaposchkin to Jesse Greenstein, May 19, 1960. Jesse Greenstein Papers, California Institute of Technology Archives, Pasadena, CA.

3.

E.W. Jenkins, From Armstrong to Nuffield: Studies in Twentieth Century Science Education in England and Wales (John Murray, London, 1979), pp. 170-214.

4.

The comment on Payne as a student is a personal communication of A. Vibert Douglas. Payne's recommendations are filed under "Gaposchkin" in the Harlow Shapley Directorial Papers, Harvard Archives, Cambridge, MA.

5.

For a fuller discussion, see P.A. Kidwell, "True Eyes and Faithful Hands: Women in British Astronomy to 1930."

6.

Martin Johnson to C. Payne-Gaposchkin, January 18, 1957. Courtesy of Kenneth Janes, Boston University, Boston, MA.

7.

C. Payne to H. Shapley, June 23, 1923. Shapley Directorial Papers. These and other letters from the Shapley Directorial Papers are cited by permission of the Harvard University Archives.

8.

C. Payne-Gaposchkin, Interview with Owen Gingerich, March 5, 1968. Niels Bohr Library, American Institute of Physics, New York, NY. This interview is quoted by permission of the Niels Bohr Library. For a fuller account of Payne-Gaposchkin's early research, see the historical introduction to Cecilia Payne-Gaposchkin: An Autobiography and Other Recollections.

9.

For the relevant papers of M.N. Saha, see Philos. Mag. **40**, 472-488 and 809-824, and Proc. R. Soc. **99A** (1921), 135-153.

10.

H. Shapley to H.N. Russell, October 25, 1923. H.N. Russell Papers, Manuscript Division, Princeton University Library, Princeton, NJ. These and other letters from the Russell Papers are quoted by permission of the Princeton University Library.

11.

H.N. Russell to H. Shapley, December 9, 1924. N.H. Russell Papers.

12.

H.N. Russell to C. Payne, January 14, 1925. N.H. Russell Papers.

13.

C. Payne to Margaret Harwood, January 9, 1925. Margaret Harwood Papers, Schlesinger Library, Radcliffe College, Cambridge, MA. This letter is quoted by permission of the Schlesinger Library.

14.

C. Payne, "Astrophysical Data Bearing on the Relative

Abundance of the Elements," Proc. Nat. Acad. Sci. U.S.A. 11 (1925), 192-198.

15.

C. Payne, Stellar Atmospheres: A Contribution to the Observational Study of High Temperatures in the Reversing Layer of Stars (Harvard Observatory, Cambridge, MA., 1925).

16.

E.F. Carpenter to H. Shapley, August 30, 1925. H. Shapley Directorial Papers.

17.

Quoted in H. Shapley to C. Payne, August 15, 1925. H. Shapley Directorial Papers.

18.

Otto Struve and Velta Zeburgs, Astronomy of the 20th Century (Macmillan, New York, 1962), p. 220.

19.

H. Shapley to H.N. Russell, August 6, 1925. H.N. Russell Papers.

20.

H. Shapley to Ada Comstock, September 14, 1928. H. Shapley Directorial Papers.

21.

E.A. Milne, Nature 116 (1925), 530.

22.

For a summary of these developments, see A Source Book in Astronomy and Astrophysics, 1900-1975, edited by K.R. Lang and O. Gingerich (Harvard University Press, Cambridge, MA., 1979), pp. 243-244.

23.

C. Payne,, Stellar Atmospheres, p. 200.

24.

Nannilou Dieter Conklin, Interview with David DeVorkin, Niels Bohr Library. This interview is quoted by permission of the Niels Bohr Library.

The Lady Wanted to Purchase a Wheatstone Bridge: Sarah Frances Whiting and Her Successor

Janet B. Guernsey

Sabrina Farm

Wellesley, Massachusetts

In the latter half of the nineteenth century, arguments raged about the education of women for anything other than wifehood and motherhood. Certainly there were isolated cases of parents, particularly fathers, who wanted their daughters to have as much "book learning" as their sons, and who recognized equal abilities among women and men. The general feeling, however, was that "woman's brain was too delicate and fragile a thing to attempt the mastery of Greek and Latin . . . ." It was said with some asperity that there would be two insane asylums and three hospitals for every women's college.[1]

Into this argument came a young man by the name of Henry Fowle Durant. His early education had been dominated by
several women whose academic abilities had made a lasting
impression on him. He had a successful and lucrative law
practice and had married his cousin, Pauline Fowle. The
birth of their first child, Harry, was followed a year later
by the birth of a daughter who lived only a short six weeks.
The hopes of the Durants then became centered on Harry. They
bought three hundred acres of land in West Needham, adjacent
to Wellesley, the estate of Horatio Hunnewell, and made
grandiose plans for Harry's future. His death from diptheria
at the age of eight was devastating. His mother fell back on
her religion for comfort, but Henry Fowle Durant, always a
lover of people and good times, found this impossible, and
he retired into a morose existence. This was terminated by a
sudden and never clearly explained conversion, after which
he and his wife decided to dedicate their efforts and wealth
to the greater glory of God.

Mr. Durant then sold his law business but remained in
control of his sizable investment portfolio. Together with
his wife, he set out to build a project for the future. The
two considered many possibilities. They visited Vassar (the

only college for women then existing), schools for young boys, and other benevolent institutions. Education was a priority interest with them. The Civil War had removed many men from the teaching profession, and yet there were few women qualified to fill the vacant positions. The Durants finally settled upon a college for women as a suitable and needed project. This was to be a school in every respect the equal of any men's college, with coverage of all disciplines, including science which was then given short shrift by many institutions of higher education.[2]

Physics and chemistry, if taught at all, were presented by the lecture method, with the professor doing demonstrations for the class. One can imagine Mr. Durant asking, "Is this way always successful? Do the experiments always work?" He was convinced that a course in physics should include laboratory work done by the students. A close friend of his, Professor Eben Horsford of Harvard, had studied under Liebig at Giessen, one of the first European universities to have student laboratories, and was convinced that this kind of study was the coming thing. An Amherst professor had said that he "could not think of having students bothering around with the equipment!"[3] But Wellesley, felt Mr. Durant, must be in the forefront of new learning methods. He did not advocate the abandonment of the classics, but insisted on the inclusion of science, with the best of equipment and teaching. "Women can do the work," he said, "I will give them the chance."[4] Then began the search for faculty, women with adequate training to fulfill his forward-looking dream. "If we are like all the colleges for men, we shall not be what we ought to be," he said.[5]

Durant's favor soon fell upon a young woman who taught mathematics and classics at a seminary in Brooklyn. Sarah Frances Whiting had been born in 1846 in Wyoming, N.Y. A descendant of pioneer settlers, she was graduated from Ingham University in 1864. Her early training was under the tutelage of her father, who had been principal of several New York academies. Miss Whiting herself was much interested in science, having helped her father set up demonstrations in "Natural Philosophy" when she was a small child.[6] Spectroscopy and photography were beginning to be understood in the early 1860s, and this young woman found them fascinating. So she was easily persuaded to accept the appointment as Professor of Physics at the new college. One problem remained, however. Mr. Durant insisted that the physics courses should include laboratory work, and Miss Whiting had no training in this area. The answer was provided by Professor Edward Pickering of MIT (then called the Institute of Technology) who had started the first student physics laboratory in the United States. Durant, who was acquainted with him, asked whether his new appointee might visit his classes and learn about laboratory equipment and procedure. Pickering, ever the gentleman, acquiesced, and Sarah Frances Whiting found herself in the first two years of her appointment commuting to Boston four days a week to study at the "Technical Institute." She mentions in her biographical notes that she was at the same time teaching mathematics (higher algebra, trigonometry, and differential calculus) at Wellesley, since "the teacher appointed to that position had failed." She was studying Pickering's two-volume _Physical Manipulations_ assiduously, making copious lists of apparatus, and asking innumerable questions about sources of supply. Everything in sight was ordered, and "everyone at Harvard, Yale, Amherst and Bowdoin helped her in making out lists." Much of the apparatus came from abroad, some from artisans who worked in the back alleys of Boston and Cambridge. Mr. Durant insisted on accompanying her on these dangerous missions, but she reports that later on she went alone!⁷

In 1878, she was ready to start. College Hall, which housed students and contained classrooms, library, and chapel, had been opened in 1876, but where was the laboratory to be located? The building was one eighth of a mile long; on the fifth floor was the organ loft and a large garret which was eventually chosen for the laboratory, with windows cut through the roof to give a view of Lake Waban. Demonstrations in optics required that the lecture room below the loft be darkened upon occasion. A system of pulleys was devised to accomplish this. Setting up the new apparatus, which had often come in many pieces, required ingenuity and mechanical skill, but Miss Whiting and Mr. Durant were undaunted and soon had everything assembled and working. Physics was required of all juniors, so classes were large, but every student worked with every piece of apparatus. Henry Fowle Durant had spared no exense, and according to the editor of Barnard's _Journal of Education_, no college he knew had a collection of physical apparatus superior to that of Wellesley.⁸

One might think that Sarah Frances Whiting had enough

to occupy her time with full classes and unfamiliar apparatus, but no! She was always on the alert for new ideas, new discoveries, and additions to her laboratory. She was aided and abetted by both Durant and Horsford. In 1876, she attended a demonstration by Alexander Graham Bell in the old Boston Music Hall where she heard (imperfectly, to be sure) a concert originating in the Concert Hall of Providence, Rhode Island. She remarked that "nothing was yet in books about the telephone, and this lecture was a great help." About this time, the English scientific journals were sprinkled with references to a new invention called a "microphone," which could "allow you to hear a fly walking." Miss Whiting went to Boston to see a demonstration, procured two samples of the device, and with the aid of Mr. Durant and a tea strainer which he had purchased for the endeavor, she set about to catch a fly. The insect was not cooperative, so the Whiting-Durant team settled for stroking the desk with a camel's hairbrush. The demonstration was nonetheless a huge success; the students were enthralled.

Professor Horsford arrived one day with a cannon ball and wanted to set up a Foucault pendulum. The whole college community watched while Sarah Frances Whiting supervised the hanging of the ball from a special suspension made to her design, with a lamp-blacked plate for recording. She says it did not work very well because of drafts, but everyone learned something. Later Horsford wanted to ventilate the chapel and the dining room, and he purchased an ozone machine for this purpose. After Miss Whiting had carefully mapped out the drafts, she "gave Mr. Ellis, who was to run the machine, a course of reading in electricity so that he would understand what he was doing." She stated with some chagrin that they had used lead pipes, forgetting what they both knew would happen: the pipes were corroded by the ozone and had to be replaced at considerable expense by pipes made of pure tin. She adds, "Mr. Horsford was more sanguine than I as to the worth of the experiment." The tin pipes were eventually sold, and the money was used to purchase an electric projection lantern. This, it seems, was a great boon, since the only lantern available was an oxyhydrogen one, used for projection of microscope slides, for polarized light demonstrations, and for outdoor stage lighting. For twenty years, she had operated this bulky lantern until "finally Miss Langford, one of the physics assistants, took it up until at last one of the men learned."

Professor Horsford wanted to put incandescent light in the lecture room, but the trustees, acquainted only with the glaring arc lights then used on railway platforms, objected that such lights would be injurious to the girls' eyes. Miss Whiting went to the Boston office of the Edison Company (she had previously lunched with Thomas Edison in New York and been shown his factory). She talked with the office manager and procured samples of every lamp then made. Trustees, faculty, and assorted students were invited to a demonstration. After spending half a day making up forty nitric acid cells to run it, she turned on an arc light, allowed the assembled guests to become uncomfortable in the glare, and then showed the incandescent lamps, mellow by contrast. The trustees were impressed and approved the project.

Mr. Durant thought that more students in the secondary schools should learn how to use microscopes. At his behest, classes in their use and theory were instituted for teachers. This led to the formation of a microscope society for the students, which later became the scientific society of the college. Many eminent scientists gave lectures on a host of subjects. Miss Whiting, of course, was pressed into service to teach the fundamentals of microscopy, not only to the school teachers, but also to the biologists who wished to use the instruments, too. The Microscopical Society of Boston was entertained, and several scientific shows were offered for the general public.

Miss Whiting was invited to join the New England Meteorological Society, the sole woman to be so honored. She quickly recognized the need for a course in this field and set about initiating one. An anemometer, thermometers, rain gauges, and other such equipment were purchased, and soon she found herself a "voluntary observer," since there was no government weather station in the vicinity. For ten years, reports, largely from data collected by students trained to read the instruments, were submitted to the U.S. Weather Bureau. With the construction of the Blue Hill Observatory, Wellesley's responsibilities ceased, but friendly relations with the staff at Blue Hill continued for many years.

Teaching was a top priority with the young professor, and she was anxious to have some of her students follow in her footsteps, as indeed many did. As she made her way around to lectures and exhibitions, she would inquire of her colleagues at other schools about opportunities in college teaching for young women. Frequently, the answer was that laboratory teaching, which was beginning to be the fashion, required the maintenance and perhaps the building of equipment. Surely this was not for young ladies! Undaunted, Sarah Frances Whiting went back to MIT to take a course in woodworking. Thereafter, she persuaded Horsford to purchase a lathe (driven by what he called a "two-catpower" steam engine) and insisted that any student interested in a teaching career take her course in woodworking: design and fabrication of physics apparatus.

Sarah Frances Whiting had many contacts with the outstanding physicists of her day. She visited Rowland at Johns Hopkins and admired his ruling machine. On leave in 1888, she visited Oliver Lodge in Liverpool, Lord Raleigh in Cambridge, Sylvanus Thompson and Lord Kelvin in Glasgow, and she met "that precocious young Joseph Thompson, just appointed Lord Raleigh's successor." She attended lectures at the British Association when Langley discussed the heat spectrum, when Hertz's discoveries were disclosed. She visited the laboratory of Kammerlingh Onnes the very week he succeeded in liquefying helium.

In 1895, when Roentgen's discovery was announced, she wasted no time but assembled a Crookes tube, a photographic plate, and a flat purse into which she had put a picture hook and a coin. These latter items were wrapped entirely in black cloth and exposed to the radiation from the Crookes tube. There are several versions of the story, but all agree that this indomitable young woman produced the first X-ray photographs in the United States.[9] The very familiar textbook picture of the bones of a hand wearing a heavy ring is thought to be an early X-ray of the hand of Annie Jump Cannon, a physics student at the time who later became famous as an astronomer.

In 1879, Mr. Durant had asked Miss Whiting to teach a semester course in astronomy. This assignment suited her well since she had attended many lectures in this field, and her friend, Professor Pickering, was preparing for a new position as Director of the Harvard Astronomical Observatory. She attacked her new task with enthusiasm. Students were routed from their beds in the early morning to observe the Great Comet of 1882. The December transit of Venus was watched and explained. Nighttime observations were made difficult by weather and inadequate equipment, so the ever resourceful teacher devised daytime laboratory experiments, using photographs and catalogues of celestial objects. She even published a small book of laboratory exercises,[10] the first ever on daytime laboratory experiments in astronomy.

For twenty years, she continued to teach with the aid of no more than a celestial globe and a portable 4-inch telescope. Mr. Durant had died in 1881, and funds for equipment were not easily accessible. In 1898, Miss Whiting heard of a Clark 12-inch equatorial glass telescope for sale at half price. She now worried about where to find the necessary three thousand dollars. A dinner party was arranged on Float Night (a traditional college ceremonial occasion), attended by four staff members of the Harvard Observatory along with a trustee of the college, Mrs. John Whitin of Whitinsville. The after-dinner discussion was animated and concentrated on Wellesley's urgent need of a telescope and an observatory. Later, while the gentlemen members of the party were returning to Cambridge on the streetcar, Miss Whiting was engaged in a serious conversation with Mrs. Whitin, not only about the Clark telescope, but also about a plan for an observatory and a faculty house for the Professor of Astronomy. The generous trustee suggested that the observatory be of white marble: the original owner of the telescope was S.V. White of Brooklyn, the Professor Miss Whiting, and the donor Mrs. Whitin. The plan was finally realized in 1904, and there were many smiles when the first aide was appointed--a young woman named Whiteside.[11]

Sarah Frances Whiting emerges in the history of Welles-ley College, and in physics education, as a stalwart woman, eagerly seizing any opportunity to learn and teach new theo-ries and discoveries, secure in her own ability, conversing easily with the great minds of her day. It must be remem-bered, however, that a good deal of male chauvinism pre-vailed in that period. Sir William Crookes, after showing her his laboratory and discussing the state of spectroscopy in depth, took her to his office, settled her graciously before the fire with a cup of tea, and remarked, "If all the ladies should know so much of spectroscopes, who would at-tend to the buttons and the breakfasts?" In response, she questioned why exact science and domesticity should be any more mutually exclusive than card playing, novel reading, or the study of language. To the brilliant Bowdoin professor who "never anticipated conversing with a lady on the Wheat-stone Bridge,"[12] she presumably just smiled in answer.

Still, she was quite conscious of being a woman in a man's world. She was almost alone in college teaching, "a somewhat nerve wearing experience of constantly being in places where a woman was not expected to be." She further remarked that physics was not reckoned among the "lady-like" subjects.[13]

Miss Whiting joined the American Physical Society shortly after its founding, one of fewer than a score of women among several hundred men. She tells of "German smokers" which were held in connection with the banquets of the Society. It was unthinkable for a woman to consider exposing herself to blue smoke and masculine conversation. Not until Professor Nichols of Cornell became president were ladies invited to attend the banquets, and even then they were not entirely sure of their welcome. In 1883, Miss Whiting was elected a fellow of the American Association for the Advancement of Science, one of only five women.[14]

Lest we think of Sarah Frances Whiting as existing with her head always in the clouds of scientific endeavor, let us consider this quote from the Wellesley Annals of 1883, written by an anonymous senior: "By the close of the winter term seniors looked worn out and felt the need of rejuvenation. Besides we had noticed that the freshmen but half knew the joy of childish sports. Therefore, for their benefit entirely, we made a great outlay of money invested in rubber balls with strings attached, jumping ropes, teeters . . . It was simply beautiful to view our infantile playfulness. Miss Whiting herself was so attracted by the seesaw that she tee-tered and teetered right over the edge of silent time!"[15] The physics students may have understood her interest.

Sarah Frances Whiting was a deeply religious woman, with a firm belief in immortality. Visitors to Observatory House, where she lived with her sister, were struck by the spiritual atmosphere of that home. Her profound religious views "seemed to raise her above every-day trials, so that she was always calm and serene as if upheld by some hidden source of joy and comfort." Engraved over the hearth-fire in Observatory House were the closing words of the Paradiso: "Love rules the sun in heaven, and all the stars."

In 1912, Miss Whiting was ready to retire, having served under six Wellesley presidents. She remarked that she would be leaving "the Department of Physics in a thoroughly modern condition to an able successor after thirty-seven years." At this time the trustees asked her to remain for a few more years as Director of the Observatory and Chairman of the Department of Astronomy which had been formed in 1912. She stayed in this position until 1916 when she re- tired for good and moved to Wilbraham, Massachusetts. Her only regret, she says somewhat poignantly, was that "of ne- cessity the pioneer work has been largely administrative. My successor has already made a record of research."[16]

The "able successor" was Louise Sherwood McDowell, born in the Finger Lakes district of New York in 1876, when Miss Whiting was 30 years old. Her father was one of the founders of the Grange, her mother for many years its treasurer. She was educated in the local schools and must have been an out- standing student, although she never discussed her early training. After graduating from high school, she was accept- ed by Wellesley but remained home for a year because of her father's terminal illness, and she entered Wellesley with the class of '98. Here she came under the influence of Miss Whiting; by then, physics was an elective subject, with courses in many areas. She probably took them all, and she must have done exceedingly well. After receiving her B.A. degree, she taught English and science at Northfield Seminary. Later, at the behest of one of her former classmates, she moved to Warren, Ohio, to teach science and mathematics at the high school. A sister of her mother's had left a legacy of five thousand dollars to her favorite niece, and this provided a nest egg, carefully hoarded for further education. In 1905, she was accepted as a graduate student in physics at Cornell University, no small feat for a woman in those days. She was awarded the master's degree in 1907 and the doctorate in 1909. Her pioneering research, with Ernest Merit, was in short electromagnetic waves, a field in which she worked for the rest of her life.[17]

As soon as her graduate study was completed, she returned to Wellesley as an Instructor. Here she established herself in the fifth-floor laboratories of College Hall, looking forward to both teaching and continuing her research. Surely Miss Whiting was happy to have her former student with her again, successful as a teacher, and with a reputation for research already established. Only three years later, Sarah Frances Whiting was content to leave the department she had worked so hard to establish in the hands of this competent student of hers who now became Professor and Chairman of the Department. The future seemed assured.

In the spring of Miss McDowell's first year as Chairman, disaster struck. College Hall, that magnificent example of French Second Empire architecture, caught fire in the early hours of a March morning and burned to the ground. Only the kitchen, separated from the rest of the building by a fire wall (because fires always started in kitchens), remained. There were no human casualties, but nearly everything was lost: classrooms, administrative and departmental offices, dormitories, science libraries, laboratories and equipment. The students were sent home for an early spring vacation while plans were made for temporary housing and facilities. An unbelievable three weeks later, the college reconvened in a stark wooden building, thereafter called the "Hen Coop."

For Louise McDowell, the fire was a disaster, yet she was undaunted. An electricity laboratory was set up in the trunk room of another dormitory, an optics laboratory in the Observatory, and lectures were given in the basement of a temporary building erected for Chemistry. On the four-hundred-acre campus, these buildings were far from each other and required almost superhuman vitality to be kept in order. Research was precluded, there was neither housing nor apparatus, and no money for either. Summer after summer, this enterprising professor returned to Cornell to continue the research which was so important to her, and to keep a-breast of what was happening elsewhere. After several years, the kitchen of College Hall, which was still standing, was renovated for the use of Physics and Geology, restoring some semblance of unity to the department. Still, there was very little money for new apparatus, and none for research. In spite of difficult conditions, teaching and enthusiasm for physics did not languish. During the years after the First World War, more Wellesley graduates went on for the doctor-ate than came from all other women's colleges.[18]

Space was limited in the kitchen quarters, but the student laboratories were adequately equipped, and students were introduced to anything new that came along. I remember going into a small basement room, crowded with "radio" components, to marvel at a device called a cathode-ray tube on which a sine curve was displayed--the shape of the house voltage! We set up a Lecher wire system with a high-frequency oscillator and actually measured wave lengths with a meter stick. The D.C. supply was a motor-generator set which broke down frequently or threw the cicuit breaker with a bang that rivaled the old streetcar breakers. For work that required a steady supply, we had a cart full of gravity cells. We worked and learned, with string and sealing wax augmented by new apparatus, when possible, until 1936 when a new building, Pendleton Hall, was opened for Physics and Chemistry.

Miss McDowell had very high standards and expectations, yet her seeming austerity hid a gentle and considerate nature. She would worry for hours about how to face a student who appeared to have problems, yet never shirk what she viewed as her responsibility. She was a perfectionist in demanding not only accurate results but also understandable explanations, and she was a stickler for correct English usage. I remember going to her with trepidation, bearing a transformer in a definitely melted condition, and being told, "We all make mistakes, and we admit them honestly." We learned radio from broomstick coils and Atwater Kent L-C tank circuits, but learn we did, and we never forgot.

During the First World War, Miss McDowell worked in the Radio Section of the Bureau of Standards. She contributed also in the Second World War by teaching War Management (ESMWT) courses in electronics. Courses for locally stationed Navy recruits were instituted. Quite willingly, she gave talks to clubs, schools, and church groups on radar, atomic energy, and world peace. She was the first woman member of the Institute of Radio Engineers, and one of the very few women who belonged to the Institute of Electrical and Electronics Engineers. From 1933 to 1937, she was Associate Editor of the American Journal of Physics. For four years, she served the American Association of Physics Teachers, becoming Vice President in 1943. She was a fellow of the American Association for the Advancement of Science and of the American Physical Society, and she instituted the Wellesley chapter of Sigma Xi. For a year after her retirement in 1945, she worked in the Radio Research Laboratory at Harvard.[19] In all her endeavors and in her research connections, she never let the fact that she was a woman stand in the way of her progress, nor did she ever rely on it. In her quiet and reserved way, she probably just ignored it.

Foremost among Miss McDowell's recreations was mountain climbing. She could outrace and exhaust her younger colleagues on any mountain. Once, she and a younger friend started on an eight-mile climb to the top of Mount Washington in a driving rain on a late afternoon. After two miles, her friend, very wet and more than a little discouraged, suggested they turn back. Louise McDowell declined: they would continue to the four-mile marker post, and then, if she wanted to turn back, they would. Four miles either way, and of course they continued the climb. She made her last climb at the age of seventy-six, and thereafter had to be content to travel other than on foot.

Sarah Frances Whiting and Louise Sherwood McDowell had many characteristics in common. They knew what needed to be done in their time to educate women in a field previously restricted to men. They knew where and how to enlist help when needed, and they let nothing stand in the way of achieving their goals. They undoubtedly contributed more toward the recognition of women in physics than either of them would have believed. It is interesting to note in closing that for the nearly seventy years of their combined tenure, Wellesley College had no man on the Physics faculty.

Notes

1.

Wellesley College 1895-1975: A Century of Women, edited
by Jean Glasscock (Wellesley College, Wellesly, MA,
1975), p. 8.

2.

Ibid., Chap. 1.

3.

Sarah Frances Whiting, "History of the Physics Department at Wellesley College, 1878-1912," (unpublished
manuscript). Archives of Wellesley College, Wellesley,
MA.

4.

Glasscock, op. cit., Foreword.

5.

Whiting, op. cit.

6.

Annie Jump Cannon, Popular Astronomy, 35 (10) (December
1927), Reprint.

7.

Whiting, op. cit.

8.

   Ibid.

9.

   Cannon, op. cit.

10.

   Sarah Frances Whiting, Daytime and Evening Exercises in
   Astronomy (Ginn & Co., Boston, 1912).

11.

   Cannon, op. cit.

12.

   Whiting, "History . . ."

13.

   Sarah Frances Whiting, "Whiting, Sarah Frances: The
   First Woman to Found and Develop Two Departments of
   Science, Physics and Astronomy in a College of High
   Rank," (unpublished manuscript). Archives of Wellesley
   College, Wellesley, MA.

14.

   Margaret W. Rossiter, Women Scientists in America:
   Struggles and Strategies to 1940 (Johns Hopkins University Press, Baltimore, 1982), p. 77.

15.

   Glasscock, op. cit., p. 244.

16.

Whiting, "Whiting, Sarah Frances . . ."

17.

Dorothy Weeks, private conversation.

18.

Ibid.

19.

Louise S. McDowell, "Biographical Notes," (unpublished manuscript). Archives of Wellesley College, Wellesley, MA.

Women in Physics: Today and Looking Toward the Future

Lucille B. Garmon

West Georgia College

Carrollton, Georgia

Unlike the other articles in this booklet, this one has little to say about individuals. Most of it is concerned with women scientists as a group, and the extent to which women today are participating in the scientific enterprise. While the main emphasis is on physics, there is also material dealing with women and the physical sciences in general, or even women and all sciences.

Two facets of this subject will be explored: the objective area of facts and numbers (statistics, in other words), and the subjective area of perceptions and expectations.

The role of women in physics is quantitatively small. It is small both in enrollment in degree programs and in employment. Table I, from figures published by the National Science Foundation,[1,2] Scientific Manpower Commission,[3] and the American Institute of Physics,[4] gives a breakdown by sex of recipients of bachelor's, master's, and doctor's degrees in physics awarded in the United States from 1930 to 1982. While the participation of women in physics education was considerable during the early part of this period (as it had been during the 1920s), it declined drastically thereafter and, except for a brief period during the Second World War, did not begin climbing significantly until the last decade.

The utilization of women physicists is also small. In 1978, according to the Bureau of the Census, there were 129,918 persons in this country who professionally identified themselves as physical scientists; 7.9% of them were female. Within this group, there were 31,623 physicists and astronomers; 2.6% of them were female.[5]

At a lively discussion on "Women in Physics," held at

the February 1971 meeting of the American Physical Society, Gloria Lubkin, senior editor of Physics Today, quoted the 1970 National Register of Scientific and Technical Personnel as listing 36,300 physicists, of whom 1354 (3.7%) were women, and added that the number of women in the field had remained roughly 3% since 1956. Lubkin went on to say, "The typical woman physicist has only a master's; the typical male physicist has a doctorate. . . . If a girl is interested in science, she generally doesn't turn to physics. Of all women in the natural and mathematical sciences listed in the National Register, 8% are in physics . . . their median annual salary in 1970 was $ 12,000. The median annual salary for men that year was $ 16,000."[6]

In the mid-1970s, of the nearly two million persons in the science and engineering population, about 185,000 (9%) were women. Even worse, only about 6% of the employed scientists and engineers were women. Between 1973 and 1975, the salaries of female doctoral scientists and engineers rose 8%, to a median level of $ 19,000, while the salaries of male doctoral scientists and engineers rose 11%, to a median of $ 23,500.[7]

Toward the end of the 1970s, the Science, Engineering, and Humanities Doctorates in the U.S., 1979 Profile showed 308,000 Ph.D. scientists and engineers in the U.S. work force, of whom 11% were women. Among employed doctoral scientists, 3% of those in physics and astronomy were women, as were 6% of those in chemistry, 7% of those in mathematics and computer science, and higher percentages for the life and social sciences. The overall unemployment among Ph.D. scientists and engineers was 2.8% for women, but only 0.7% for men.[8]

According to a newsletter of the Association for Women in Science, "the median annual full-time salary (in 1979) was $ 30,000 for men and $ 23,100 for women. Women had a lower salary in every field and regardless of years of experience. . . . These salary differences are even greater than was true in 1977; especially disturbing is the fact that the salary difference for the youngest men and women Ph.D. scientists is greater than it had been in 1977. This, at least, cannot be rationalized as an accumulated differential."[9]

Still another piece of discouraging news comes from the academic community, where a larger proportion of women than of men physicists are employed. In 1981, Arthur Schawlow, then President of the American Physical Society, sent a letter to each physics department in this country that offered a Ph.D., expressing concern about the "under-representation of women in the profession of physics." This concern was based on a survey prepared by Laura Eisenstein and Elizabeth Baranger for the APS Committee on the Status of Women in Physics (CSWP) of the senior faculty in physics departments. "Senior faculty" included those with the rank of assistant professor, associate professor, or professor, who were full-time or part-time in physics, but not lecturers, instructors, research or adjunct professors, emeriti, etc. All 171 Ph.D.-granting physics departments in the United States were tallied. The survey found 4,176 faculty members who fit the above description, including 79 women (<2%). The survey showed that forty institutions had only one woman among their senior staff, five had two women, one (MIT) had four women, and "the remaining 125 had no women on their senior physics faculty."[10]

Another CSWP survey in industry found no female physicists as research managers in any major industrial laboratory, though there were several women among their senior staff physicists.[11]

If we take a second look at Table I, we can see that the numbers are getting better. From a low around 1950, the percentage of women has been increasing. A bit of additional information that can be obtained from data such as these is the relative number of physicists who go on for a graduate degree. Table II compares the numbers of bachelor's degrees in physics, at five-year intervals since 1950, to the number of master's degrees two years later and the number of doctoral degrees six years later. The rate of procuring a master's degree has seesawed between the sexes, with no big changes for either since the mid-1950s. But by the late 1970s women were almost three times as likely as they had been twenty-five years earlier to get a Ph.D., the "union card" in physics.

In the physical sciences as a whole, the percentage of doctoral degrees earned by women has also increased. The decade of the 1970s was the first in which the percentage of doctorates granted to women matched or exceeded the levels of the 1920s. This was true in all fields of science. Table III gives the numerical percentages and shows also the percentages for other areas of science and for engineering. The participation of women has increased most steeply in the fields in which they have traditionally been underrepresented. The percentage of women among the engineering Ph.D.s, for instance, has gone up approximately tenfold since 1970.[12]

An additional fact is that, while the number of Ph.D.s in science and engineering awarded to women has increased steadily since 1971, the number awarded to men has declined. From 341 doctorates awarded to women in the physical sciences in 1971, the number has increased by an average of about 4% per year; from 5,398 doctorates awarded to men in the physical sciences in 1971, the number has decreased by an average of about 4% a year.[10] (The precise percentages are such that, in the unlikely event these trends continue, the year 2005 will see more Ph.D. degrees in the physical sciences awarded to women than to men!)

The representation of women in U.S. science and engineering facilities was up from 9.3% in 1977 to 10.9% in 1981. After controlling for rank, salary differentials for academic men and women physicists were only 3% in 1981; that is, women in physics departments averaged 97% of the salaries of men with the same rank.

While women account for only 5% of all Ph.D.-level industrial personnel, the number of female scientists and engineers in industry who hold doctorates doubled between 1977
and 1981. New women Ph.D.s now plan industrial employment at
about the same rate as men. The increase in the number of
women with doctoral degrees seeking employment in the private sector is a new development. In 1981, median salaries
in industry for women scientists who had obtained their
Ph.D.s in 1979-90 were 96% as much as for their male coun-
terparts.[12]

Table IV shows some average starting salaries for baccalaureate scientists, as reported by the Scientific Manpower Commission[13] and the American Chemical Society.[14] The
figures are typical of the male/female comparison among scientists just entering the work force. There is still a gen-
der gap among experienced scientists, with women being paid
less on the average than men, but there has been a big improvement over the 75% of men's salaries that women scientists were earning in 1970.

Finally, Table V shows that young women are participating to a significantly greater extent in professional scientific organizations than their older compatriots. The percentage of women in the American Physical Society (whose membership is 83% Ph.D.s) is much less still than in the American Chemical Society (45% Ph.D.s), but in both organizations, youngest members include a substantially larger fraction of women than the general membership.

For more extensive documentation on the vastly increased, but still minority participation of women in the scientific enterprise, see references such as Vetter[15] and Kistiakowsky.[16]

Let us now take a look at how perceptions of society toward women physicists and expectations of women toward their chances of having a satisfying career in physics have been changing.

In 1980, Vera Kistiakowsky published in **Physics** Today the article "Women in Physics: Unnecessary, Injurious, and out of Place?" The title was taken from an essay of Strindberg's, written in the late 19th century in opposition to the appointment of a woman mathematician to a professorship at the University of Stockholm and attempting to prove "as decidedly as that two and two make four, what a monstrosity is a woman who is a professor of mathematics, and how unnecessary, injurious and out of place she is."[16] In comparison with sentiments such as these, the atmosphere today seems pretty good indeed.

In 1971, the panel discussion on "Women in Physics," referred to earlier in this paper, took place. In addition to Gloria Lubkin, the panelists included Enid Sichel, Betsy Ancker-Johnson, Chien-Shiung Wu, Charles Townes, D. Allan Bromley, and Henriette Faraggi, then President-Elect of the French Physical Society. The panel was moderated by Fay Aj-zenberg-Selove. Discussed were statistics, whether there was a need for women in physics, what obstacles there were to women entering and maintaining careers in physics, and some personal horror stories.

The question of the need for women in physics was treated more or less predictably. Nobody in 1971 was about to say that a woman in physics was an unnatural monstrosity. Wu said, "Men have always dominated the fields of science and technology. Look what environmental mess we are in. . . . Women's vision and humane concern may be exactly what is needed in our society."[6]

Among the problems and obstacles cited were societal discouragement, lack of role models to young women considering careers in physics, discrimination by graduate schools against women, difficulties in arranging child care for women who wanted to combine scientific careers with families, and difficulties in reentry for women who wanted to drop out for a while to raise children. Sichel noted that media coverage of successful women scientists tended to suggest that they all had five lovely children, were terrific cooks and housekeepers, and possessed a myriad of other talents. This, she said, certainly discouraged most women from seeking an active scientific career, although she admitted that the Superwoman image might sometimes be true.[6]

Ancker-Johnson said that the worst prejudice she encountered was in job hunting, when she was offered second-rate positions because employers had decided that she belonged to an undependable subset of physicists: A woman will marry, and what is invested in her goes down the drain. She also added that while pregnant, she was laid off over her protest and was not even allowed to enter the building for three months prior to the birth to hear a talk or get a book from her private collection without special permission.[6]

Some of this meeting's horror stories originated right there. When the inspiration of Marie Curie as a role model was brought up, a prominent male physicist in the audience commented that the image of Marie Curie had been exaggerated and that, if he had been married to Pierre Curie, he would have been Madame Curie, too.[6]

That session inspired a letter cosigned by twenty women physicists, requesting that the APS Council establish a committee on women to study their situation and make appropriate recommendations. At the time, the assembling of concrete data on the status of women in physics was a novel enterprise. Kistiakowsky recalls that she was approached by an eminent male physicist and asked why the Committee on Women in Physics was wasting its time on a study when there were only two women physicists in the United States and both of them were happy.[16]

There is probably a principle in a psychology textbook somewhere (if not, there should be one!) that describes the effect on attitudes of avoiding the consequences of one's behavior. However egregious and reprehensible the policies and practices of those in power may be, if over a period of time the exercise of such practices brings them rewards rather than retribution, then the power elite develops the attitude that those policies, far from being in any way wrong, are in fact right, fitting, and proper, and perhaps even necessary for the smooth functioning of society. This was, for instance, the case with local laws on racial segregation which were once considered right, fitting, and proper in many parts of this country. Since the civil rights movement and enforcement of desegregation rulings, attitudes have changed. Overt racial discrimination is not considered acceptable anymore, and few public officials are heard expressing racist sentiments.

The women's movement has frequently been compared with the civil rights movement, and some of the same attitude changes as a result of new statutory rulings and their enforcement can be traced.

Since the early 1970s, "Affirmative Action" and "Equal Opportunity" have become bywords for employers. Laws, court rulings, and executive orders have made baseless sexual discrimination much less acceptable. Probably no employer today would tell a qualified female applicant, "We've decided not to hire women for responsible positions. There's too much risk they'd quit to raise kids." It is not acceptable today to be overtly antifemale anymore.

Have the Equal Employment Opportunity Commission, Executive Orders 11246 and 11375 (barring discrimination against women in federally assisted programs), the feminist renaissance, and so forth made a difference? In her 1980 article, Kistiakowsky reviewed the situation and its recent developments. Prior to 1971, according to her, the situation for women physicists was little changed from the period before 1920. She then commented on changing attitudes during the 1970s:

Societal views of appropriate roles for women are changing. Every pre-teenage girl today knows that there are women in many "men's" fields, including the physical sciences, and gradually this should result in increases in the numbers of girls who take physical science and advanced math in high school and who can therefore consider such majors in college. . . . Our society is now one in which the majority of women are employed outside of the home for a major part of their adult lives; [so realization of the options] should lead to much more substantial numbers of young women laying the foundation in high school and college for graduate work in physics. . . . Anecdotal evidence indicates that negative peer attitudes concerning the appropriateness of scientific careers for women were an important factor in so few women going on for the doctorate in physics, together with the perception that job opportunities were limited for doctorate-level women. Bluntly, why get a Ph.D. in physics when you can't get an interesting job and it makes it harder to be married? . . . Here again, changing attitudes concerning the appropriate roles for women and the changing views of marriage must also have improved the general situation in the last ten years. Furthermore, affirmative action, ineffective as it has been on the

whole, has created the impression that doctoral
women scientists can get jobs. It comes then as no
surprise that more women now continue to a doctorate.[16]

In response to an inquiry on whether the belief that
women scientists can now get jobs is an "impression" only,
Kistiakowsky replied, "It is my impression that doctoral
women scientists still are judged against models based on
previous scientists which incorporate masculine characteristics as those necessary for success in science. Therefore,
employment is still different for women than for men. However, the situation has improved by orders of magnitude from
outright 'won't hire' to a real willingness to hire if the
candidate comes close enough to the model."[17]

A further example of changed perceptions of what is
acceptable today comes from an article called "What Is Science" that appeared in The Physics Teacher in 1969. The
author, a Nobel prizewinning male physicist, spoke of once
overhearing one girl explaining to another how to make a
straight line while knotting argyle socks and learning a
lesson: "The female mind is capable of understanding analyt-

ical geometry. Those people who have for years been insisting (in the face of all obvious evidence to the contrary) that the male and female are equally capable of rational thought may have something. The difficulty may just be that we have never yet discovered a way to communicate with the female mind. If it is done in the right way, you may be able to get something out of it."[18]

When asked whether there had been any repercussions to the antifemale bias of the article, the editor replied that there had not, and no one on the staff had at the time noticed anything blatantly sexist about the tone of the article. If run today, however, the article would probably produce outrage.[19]

Recently, some of the women who participated in the 1971 panel on "Women in Physics" have responded to requests to comment on how they feel attitudes have changed since then. Fay Ajzenberg-Selove wrote:

> I suspect that all women of my generation
> were subject to discrimination; this is certainly
> true of the women I know, including myself. I

think that there is considerably less discrimination in _junior_ positions in academic institutions
and government laboratories now, thanks to the
affirmative action guidelines and to the presence
of more women in these places. . . .

The APS has changed greatly. In 1970 no women
had been Presidents of the APS nor served on its
Council. Since then C.S. Wu and Mildred Dressel-
haus have been _elected_ to be President and there
are always women elected to the Council. . . . The
APS used to have "Women's Programs" at APS meet-
ings for the wives of male members. A few of us
were outraged by this over the years, and when we
finally had women members of the Council, this was
changed to "Companion Programs" or the like, and
this change also occurred in international meet-
ings after some time. (It does not seem like a big
issue, but it appeared to us to be a subliminal
message that women were guests rather than partic-
ipants in Physics.)[20]

Enid Sichel wrote:

Tremendous progress has been made in removing barriers to women in entry level physics jobs in industry, government, and universities. The progress is the result of legal action, federal guidelines and affirmative action. . . . It is still _very_ difficult and rare for women to be promoted to higher levels in physics. Job mobility is a pressing problem in some geographical areas. It seems as if many women students today are undaunted by the prospects of career plus family responsibilities. I don't really know if in fact women cope with the problems today more easily than 12 years ago, but there seems to be a dramatic change in expectations.[21]

In other words, apparently more women today think that yes, they can be Superwomen.

Some important conclusions were recently summarized by the Committee on the Education and Employment of Women in Science and Engineering:

The most striking change that has taken place

since 1977 is the growth in numbers of doctoral women scientists. In just four years, the total supply of women Ph.D.s in science and engineering increased by 50 percent. . . . There are (in academe) signs that the increases in numbers of women scientists among junior faculty that took place between 1973 and 1977 are now being reflected at the associate professor rank. . . . For female assistant professors the salary deficits in several fields have diminished or essentially disappeared since 1977. . . . (In industry), that recent women graduates are planning industrial employment at the same rate as men is a new phenomenon. By all indications, these younger women scientists believe that their place in the business and industry sector is both wanted and appropriate.[12]

The newly enhanced and expanded role for women in physics is not reflected in a glamorous-looking female physicist being recently profiled in an advertisement for a popular brand of Scotch. And it is not just that Sally Ride (a Ph.D. physicist) captured America's imagination by being the first

U.S. woman in space. Rather, the current atmosphere is sending a message to young women with ability and interest in physics, mathematics, engineering, and computer science. And the message is, "Go for it!" Good luck.

Notes

1.

National Science Foundation, The Stock of Science and Enineering Master's Degree Holders in the United States (NSF 81-307) (Government Printing Office, Washington, D.C., 1981), p. 27. Data given as "estimated."

2.

National Science Foundation, Science and Engineering Degrees: 1950-1980: A Source Book (NSF 82-307) (Government Printing Office, Washington, D.C., 1982), p. 36. Sources of data given as the National Science Foundation and the National Center for Educational Statistics, Department of Education.

3.

Scientific Manpower Commission, Manpower Comments 19

(10), 22 (1982). Data credited to the National Center for Educational Statistics.

4.

Susanne D. Ellis, AIP Report: Manpower Statistics Division, AIP Pub. No. R-151.20 (February, 1983), p. 7. Data collected directly from degree-granting physics departments.

5.

Bureau of the Census, Selected Characteristics of Persons in Physical Science: 1978 (Special Studies Series P-23, No. 108) (Government Printing Office, Washington, D.C., 1980), p. 7.

6.

Gloria B. Lubkin, Phys. Today 24 (4), 23-27 (1971).

7.

National Science Board, Science Indicators 1976 (Government Printing Office, Washington, D.C., 1977), pp. 152-154.

8.

Commission of Human Resources, Science, Engineering, and Humanities Doctorates in the U.S.: 1979 Profile (National Academy Press, Washington, D.C., 1980).

9.

Barbara Filner, Newsletter, Association for Women in Science 10 (6), 4 (1980/81).

10.

APS news staff, Phys. Today 35 (2), 99 (1982).

11.

Enid Sichel, as reported in CSWP Gazette 9, 3-5 (March 1, 1983).

12.

Committee on the Education and Employment of Women in Science and Engineering, National Research Council, Climbing the Ladder: An Update on the Status of Doctoral Women Scientists and Engineers (National Academy of Science, Washington, D.C., 1983), pp. 2.5, 4.6, and 5.6.

13.

Scientific Manpower Commission, Salaries of Scientists, Engineers, and Technicians: A Summary of Salary Surveys, 9th ed. (American Association for the Advancement of Science, Washington, D.C., 1979), p. 13; 10th ed. (1982), pp. 11, 13.

14.

American Chemical Society, Chemical and Engineering

News <u>60</u> (42), 49-50; <u>61</u> (27) 33-37 (1983).

15.

Betty M. Vetter, Science <u>214</u>, 1313-1321 (1981).

16.

Vera Kistiakowsky, Phys. Today <u>33</u> (2), 32-40 (1980).

17.

Vera Kistiakowsky, private communication, May 13, 1983.

18.

Richard Feynman, Phys. Teach. <u>7</u>, 315 (1969).

19.

Clifford Schwartz, private conversation, June 1983.

20.

Fay Ajzenberg-Selove, private communication, May 2, 1983.

21.

Enid Sichel, private communication, April 28, 1983.

Table I. Physics degrees conferred in the U.S. by level and sex: 1930-1982.

Year	Bachelor's			Master's			Doctor's		
	Men	Women	Percent[a]	Men	Women	Percent[a]	Men	Women	Percent[a]
1930[b]	799	211	21%	184	34	16%	103	6	5.5%
1935	920	185	17%	218	26	11%	129	2	1.5%
1940	1,336	223	14%	319	32	9.1%	129	3	2.3%
1945	749	226	23%	172	29	14%	39	8	17%
1950[c]	3,287	127	3.7%	888	34	3.7%	353	5	1.4%
1955	1,920	76	3.8%	701	28	3.8%	499	12	2.3%
1960	4,166	172	4.0%	1,038	35	3.3%	477	10	2.1%
1965	4,708	246	5.0%	1,826	80	4.2%	922	20	2.1%
1970	5,004	329	6.2%	2,047	158	7.2%	1,402	37	2.6%
1971	4,733	343	6.0%	2,042	152	6.9%	1,439	43	2.9%
1972	4,322	323	7.0%	1,876	159	7.8%	1,301	43	3.2%
1973	3,955	313	7.3%	1,642	113	6.4%	1,287	51	3.8%
1974	3,625	337	8.5%	1,526	136	8.2%	1,063	47	4.2%
1975	3,354	362	9.7%	1,453	124	7.9%	1,028	52	4.8%
1976	3,156	388	11%	1,319	132	9.1%	952	45	4.5%
1977	3,062	358	10%	1,193	126	9.6%	890	55	5.8%
1978	2,961	369	11%	1,171	123	9.5%	824	49	5.6%
1979	2,939	399	12%	1,184	135	10%	852	66	7.2%
1980	2,963	434	13%	1,074	118	9.9%	767	63	7.6%
1981[d]	3,008	433	13%	1,179	115	8.9%	805	61	7.0%
1982[e]	4,025	533	12%	1,312	164	11%	849	63	6.9%

[a] Degrees to women as percent of total, rather than as percent of degrees to men.

[b] Source for years 1930-1945: Reference 1.

[c] Source for years 1950-1980: Reference 2.

[d] Source for year 1981: Reference 3.

[e] Source for year 1982: Reference 4. These figures are for the academic year 1981-82 (July 1 to June 30) as reported to the American Institute of Physics by degree-granting physics departments. For comparison with other entries above, this source reports a total of 4,513 bachelor's degrees in physics granted during 1980-81 and a total of 4,440 during 1979-80.

Table II. Percent of baccalaureate physicists acquiring advanced degrees.

Bacca-laureate class	Percent obtaining master's degree two years later		Percent obtaining doctor's degree six years later	
	Men	Women	Men	Women
1950	26%	27%	14%	6%
1955	42%	37%	29%	8%
1960	34%	36%	23%	12%
1965	43%	39%	31%	17%
1970	41%	48%	19%	14%
1975	36%	35%	24%	17%
1980	44%	38%	---	---

Source: Data in Reference 2 and Table I.

Table III. Percent of all science and engineering doctorates which were
awarded to women: 1970-1981

Year	Total science and engineering	Physical sciences (including math/comp. sci.)	Engin- eering	Life science	Social science
1970	9.1%	5.7%	0.4%	12.8%	16.1%
1971	10.2%	5.9%	0.4%	14.1%	17.8%
1972	11.2%	6.6%	0.6%	14.8%	18.8%
1973	13.0%	7.2%	1.4%	17.3%	21.0%
1974	14.3%	7.7%	1.0%	17.9%	23.4%
1975	15.8%	8.3%	1.7%	19.4%	24.8%
1976	16.8%	9.0%	1.9%	19.7%	26.3%
1977	18.0%	9.8%	2.8%	20.1%	28.1%
1978	19.6%	10.5%	2.2%	22.1%	30.2%
1979	21.1%	11.5%	2.5%	23.5%	33.0%
1980	22.6%	12.2%	3.6%	25.2%	34.6%
1981	23.4%	12.0%	3.9%	26.4%	35.6%

Source: Data in Reference 12.

Table IV. Some representative median annual starting salaries of baccalaureate physicists and chemists, by sex.

	Men	Women	Women's salary as percent of men
Physicists in industry (manufacturing)			
1977-78[a]	$15,500	$15,400	99.1%
1980[b]	$19,900	$20,100	101%
Physicists in government (civilian)			
1977-78[a]	$12,300	$13,000	106%
1980[b]	$14,000	$17,900	128%
Chemists (all employers)			
1975[b]	$10,000	$9,600	96%
1978[b]	$12,500	$13,000	104%
1981[c]	$18,000	$19,000	105%
1983[d]	$20,400	$20,500	101%

[a] Reference 13, 9th edition.

[b] Reference 13, 10th edition.

[c] Reference 14, 1982.

[d] Reference 14, 1983. For comparison, the salaries reported for experienced women chemists averaged 85% of those of men.

Table V. Percent of women among members of the American Physical Society and the American Chemical Society, by age.

American Physical Society		American Chemical Society	
Age of members	Percent who are women	Age of members	Percent who are women
27 and under	9%	21-25	32%
28-32	7%	26-30	25%
33-37	5%	31-35	16%
38 and over	3.3%	36-65	9%
		over 65	1%
all ages	4%	all ages	12%

Sources: Private communication with officers of APS and ACS.

Biographical Information

<u>Lucille</u> <u>B.</u> <u>Garmon</u> received her B.S. and M.S. degrees in chemistry from the University of Richmond, and her Ph.D., also in chemistry, from the University of Virginia. She has spent more time teaching physics than chemistry, however, first at Auburn University and now at West Georgia College where she holds the position of Professor of Physics in addition to serving as Acting Chairman of the Chemistry Department. Her professional interests include history and philosophy of science and science education in general. Her interest in women's scientific history transcends academic disciplines.

<u>Janet</u> <u>B.</u> <u>Guernsey</u> received her B.A. degree in physics from Wellesley College, and her M.A. degree in engineering science and applied physics from Harvard University. Her doctorate, in nuclear physics, was awarded by MIT in 1955. She taught at Wellesley College from 1942 to 1978, the last eleven years as Chairman of the Physics Department and as Louise S. McDowell Professor of Physics. She has been active in the American Association of Physics Teachers on the re-

gional and national levels, serving as the organization's president in 1975. Her publications include several articles and a book chapter on neutron scattering.

Peggy Aldrich Kidwell earned an undergraduate degree in physics from Grinnell College. She obtained her doctorate in the history of science from Yale University. She is presently a Postdoctoral Fellow at the National Museum of American History of the Smithsonian Institution where she is working on a biography of Cecilia Payne-Gaposchkin.

Katherine Russell Sopka got her B.A. and M.A. degrees in physics from Radcliffe College. Her Ph.D. in education and the history of science was awarded by Harvard University in 1976, based on her dissertation "Quantum Physics in America 1920 - 1935" which was published in book form by Arno Press in 1980. She has taught at Kean State College and at the University of Colorado in Boulder. At present, she is Assistant Professor of Physics at Fort Lewis College in Durango, Colorado. Her research interests focus on the conceptual development in the physical sciences, the rise of physics in the United States, and the training and career development of women physicists.

Sallie A. Watkins earned her B.S. in chemistry from Notre Dame College in Cleveland, Ohio. Her M.S. in physics was awarded by the Catholic University of America where she also obtained her Ph.D. in physics in 1958. After teaching in high schools in the Cleveland area, at Notre Dame College, and at the Catholic University of America, she is now Professor of Physics at the University of Southern Colorado. Her professional activities include work on the regional and national levels for the American Association of Physics Teachers on whose Executive Board and Publications Committee she is presently serving. In addition, she is a member of the American Physical Society Forum on Physics and Society. Her interest in the history of physics is reflected in several articles she has published in professional journals.